The
Supreme Court
of Canada Decision on
ABORTION

The Supreme Court
of Canada Decision on
ABORTION

Edited by Shelagh Day & Stan Persky

New Star Books
Vancouver
1988

Commentary © 1988 by Shelagh Day
Introduction © 1988 by Stan Persky

Canadian Cataloguing in Publication Data

Main entry under title:
The Supreme Court of Canada decision on abortion

 Bibliography: p.
 ISBN 0-919573-85-1

 1. Abortion — Law and legislation — Canada.
I. Day, Shelagh. II. Persky, Stan, 1941-   III. Canada.
Supreme Court.
KE8920.A47S96 1988   344.71'0419   C88-091400-9

Editor for the press: Rolf Maurer
Cover design: Fiona MacGregor

The publisher is grateful for support provided by the
Canada Council, Writing and Publication Section, and
the Department of Communications, Book Publishing
Industry Development Program.

Printed and bound in Canada by Imprimerie Gagné,
Louiseville, Qué.
1 2 3 4 5   92 91 90 89 88

New Star Books Ltd.
2504 York Avenue
Vancouver, B.C.
Canada V6K 1E3

Contents

Introduction

Ottawa, January 28, 1988: The Supreme Court of Canada Decision on Abortion

The highest court in the land had deliberated for almost sixteen months. At issue was one of the most contentious, passionately felt, and difficult-to-decide problems that the Supreme Court of Canada had tackled in its 112-year history: the relationship between abortion and the law. Beyond a strictly legal verdict, the decision would have implications fundamental to the nation for matters involving morality, social philosophy, and women's equality.

While the Court would definitively rule on the fate of three doctors — the most prominent of them being Dr. Henry Morgentaler — charged with conspiracy to perform abortions, and would determine the legality of Canada's nearly 20-year-old abortion law — section

251 of the Criminal Code — its judgment could also touch on a wide array of related issues directly affecting how Canadians live together. While its opinions on these latter questions could hardly be expected to be exhaustive, the Court was likely to say something significant about the Canadian Constitution, and especially section 7 of the Charter of Rights and Freedoms which guarantees Canadians "the right to life, liberty and security of the person. . ." In so doing, the Court would at least be indicating the extent of individual rights with respect to the sanctity of our bodies and, in particular, women's right to control their own bodies, as well as the limits to be placed on the state in interfering with those rights.

In addition, the Court most probably would be considering questions of fairness, equality of access, and just procedures in the operation of the existing abortion law. As well, the justices could, if they chose, offer suggestions about the status of the foetus and the proper public forum for determining that status.

Given the potential scope of the decision, when it was announced toward the end of January, 1988 that the Supreme Court would render its judgment on Thursday, January 28, it was no surprise that intense national scrutiny turned to the august body of red-robed justices who had pondered the case ever since Dr. Henry Morgentaler appealed to the Court in October 1986. In fact, the Court had not attracted this degree of attention since 1981 when it had been asked to give its opinion on whether a new Canadian constitution could be established solely by Parliament or whether such an act required the concurrence of the provinces. Certainly, since the passage of the Constitution Act in 1982, no case invoking the power of the constitution's pivotal Charter of Rights and Freedoms promised such legal significance or public impact.

Ostensibly, there were two sets of immediate

principal actors in the drama. Making the landmark decision: Supreme Court Chief Justice Brian Dickson and six of his colleagues on the nine-member Court who had heard the case. And the appellants: Henry Morgentaler, his two fellow physicians, Leslie Smoling and Robert Scott, and their lawyer, Morris Manning.

But in a more profound sense, this was to be a judgment about the status of women in Canada. More than 60,000 Canadian women annually sought and received abortions, but because of the symbolic significance that attached to the debate, and the quite literal and intimate issue of who would have primary control over what had come to be known as "reproductive rights", it affected all Canadian women.

That, at least, was the way many women saw it. Of course, not everyone agreed, especially a vociferous minority of anti-abortionists who had organized under the banner of "pro-life". In a debate so polarized that the very language and terms in which it is conducted are themselves at issue — whether one uses, for example, the words "foetus" or "unborn child" serves to immediately declare a position — determining the true subjects of the Court decision is no trivial matter. That opposition aside, however, few could deny that this would be a verdict that directly affected and engaged the attention of millions of women in Canada.

The Morgentaler Cases, 1970-1988

When Henry Morgentaler arrived at the Supreme Court in Ottawa on January 28, 1988 to receive the decision of the justices, it marked the last legal step in an almost two-decade-old mission undertaken by the 64-year-old doctor whose clipped white beard and hawk-nosed profile had made him a familiar figure, even a symbol, in Canada's abortion debate. In the past fifteen years, he had been acquitted at four trials, seen two of those jury acquittals overturned by higher courts, served ten months in prison, and had emerged to resist the efforts of successive Canadian governments to shut down his abortion clinics in three provinces, and to stand before the nation's highest court. His opponents had charged him with being a monster, and worse. An even larger number of people revered his courage and integrity. In either case, he was, by any standards, a remarkable person.

Born in Lodz, Poland in 1923, his father was Josef Morgentaler, a trade union leader in the city's textile industry. Though nominally Jewish, "the desire for social justice," Henry Morgentaler has remarked, "was, in practice, the religion in which I grew up." When he was sixteen, his father was murdered by the Gestapo shortly after the German army occupied Poland in 1939. Five years later, in 1944, the remaining Jews of Lodz were shipped to the Nazi death camp at Auschwitz. His mother, Golda Morgentaler, died there; Henry and his brother Michael survived the Holocaust. Inspired by his concentration camp ordeal and family tragedy to devote himself to alleviating human suffering, Morgentaler studied medicine, first in West Germany and later in Canada at the University of Montreal. He became a doctor in 1955. Certainly, Morgentaler's formative experiences give pause to those taking the measure of the brutal accusations later to be hurled at him by his more extreme opponents in the abortion debate.

It was not until 1967 that Morgentaler first made public what would be his most contentious belief. Appearing before a parliamentary committee studying Canada's abortion laws, the Montreal doctor told MP's that abortion ought to be seen "not as a privilege but as a right." It would prove to be a fateful declaration. Women began phoning his general practice clinic seeking abortions. "It wasn't enough to say the law should be changed," Morgentaler later recalled. "I felt it was my duty as a doctor to provide help, despite the risks." Shortly afterwards, he performed his first abortion.

In 1969, the Canadian Parliament passed a new abortion law. Although less restrictive than previous legislation, section 251 of the Criminal Code, as it was called, was nonetheless a curious combination of "crime and exception", as a Toronto *Globe and Mail* editorial described it: "The crime was procuring an abortion; the exception applied to women whose life or health was likely to be endangered by being denied one." The law set out an elaborate mechanism for procuring a legal abortion which required that *a)* a therapeutic abortion committee consisting of not less than three doctors *b)* at an "accredited or approved" hospital at which the abortion was to be performed *c)* issue a written certificate stating that continuation of the pregnancy would be likely to endanger the woman's "life or health". The obvious difficulties and delays caused by that law are fully examined in the Supreme Court of Canada decision on abortion and need not be addressed here. More to the point for our purposes, Dr. Morgentaler found the law dangerously unreasonable and continued to perform abortions outside of an accredited hospital and without the required certificate from therapeutic abortion committees.

The Montreal police raided Morgentaler's clinic in June 1970 and charged him with conspiracy to perform an abortion. It was but the first act of what would turn out to be a lengthy courtroom drama. We noted above that while the 1988 Supreme Court decision would immediately affect Morgentaler and his colleagues, it would be a mistake not to understand that the real impact of the judgment would be primarily upon the lives of Canadian women. It would be equally misleading to assume that the series of trials that would bring Morgentaler to the Supreme Court in 1988 occurred in a political vacuum.

Although the history is voluminously documented elsewhere, we must note here that, in a strong sense, what made the political struggles around the Morgentaler cases possible was the emergence at this time of the contemporary women's movement.

To cite just one instance: as early as 1970, the same year in which Morgentaler was first charged, the Vancouver Women's Caucus spearheaded the first cross-country demonstration against what it regarded as the utter inadequacy of the newly-legislated section 251. The Abortion Caravan, as this national demonstration was known, travelled across the country, arousing awareness of the issue and gathering supporters as it went. Its two-day demonstration by a 400-member contingent on Parliament Hill in Ottawa, including a dramatic moment in which protesters entered the parliamentary gallery and chained themselves to the railing, established the first links of a modern coast-to-coast feminist network in Canada. In subsequent years, it was this movement which would provide the bulk of material support for Morgentaler's defence as well as a massive program of political education on the abortion question.

Before the first Morgentaler case was heard more than three years later, a dozen further charges were laid. In November 1973, however, a Montreal jury of eleven men and one woman acquitted Morgentaler. Rather than ending the legal controversy, the jury's decision was only the beginning of a tangled courtroom odyssey. A half-year later, in April 1974, the Quebec Court of Appeal overturned the acquittal, found Morgentaler guilty, and ordered him to appear for sentencing. Morgentaler then turned to the Supreme Court of Canada, but it upheld the Quebec Court of Appeal action in March 1975, and the doctor entered Montreal's Bordeaux Jail to begin serving an 18-month sentence.

Three months later, in June 1975, Morgentaler was

brought before a second jury on new charges. Again, he was acquitted, but returned to prison to continue serving his sentence. Meanwhile, the appeal court reversal of a jury verdict prompted the federal government to introduce an amendment to the Criminal Code to prevent appeal courts from reversing jury verdicts and, instead, limiting their power to ordering a new trial. In January 1976, after serving ten months, Morgentaler was released on bail, pending his new trial on the original charges. The case was retried in Montreal in September 1976, and once again resulted in acquittal. Shortly afterwards, the new Parti Quebecois provincial government, elected in November 1976, barred further prosecutions of Morgentaler by declaring that the federal abortion law was unworkable. In fact, the Quebec government of Premier Rene Levesque created a network of abortion clinics throughout the province within the next few years and even hired Dr. Morgentaler to train other doctors in abortion techniques.

The personal costs of the legal ordeal had been considerable: Morgentaler had suffered a heart attack while in prison; at the end of the Quebec prosecutions, he was $100,000 in debt; his private relations had suffered as well. He withdrew from the main venues of the abortion debate for several years.

In 1983, his health restored, and his debts paid off, Morgentaler returned to the fray by opening clinics in Winnipeg and Toronto at a time when the resurgent anti-abortion lobby had persuaded numerous hospitals throughout the country to abandon the procedure. Once again, it's necessary to note the political context in which the new clinics were established. The country had experienced in 1981-82 an often unsatisfactory debate that resulted in the Constitution Act of 1982. One of the more striking features of this debate was a national and successful campaign by the women's movement to secure in the constitution guarantees that the rights and freedoms enshrined in that document applied equally to women and men. Invigorated by its legislative triumph, the women's movement was in a position, in 1983, to encourage new resistance to the forces seeking to further limit women's access to abortion procedures. Morgentaler's initiative in opening clinics in Ontario and Manitoba at that time, then, is perhaps best understood as a feature of the altered political circumstances shaped by the women's movement rather than as an isolated event.

In any case, and in short order, Morgentaler and his colleagues were in legal trouble. In June 1983 he was charged in Winnipeg, and a month later similar charges were laid against Morgentaler and two other doctors in Toronto.

The case came before a Toronto jury in November 1984, about a year-and-a-half after the charges had been laid. The jury acquitted all three doctors. For Morgentaler, it was his fourth jury acquittal on abortion charges. Again, it was not over. The Crown appealed. In October 1985, the Ontario Court of Appeal overturned the acquittals and ordered a new trial. Although Morgentaler once more appealed to the Supreme Court of Canada, legal observers saw the Ontario Court of Appeal's 169-page judgment as a particularly ominous turn of events for the defence, as appeal court decisions are seldom interfered with by higher tribunals.

Two kinds of arguments had been made before the Ontario appeal court — non-constitutional ones and, in the wake of the 1982 Constitution Act, arguments that the abortion law violated various sections of the Charter of Rights and Freedoms. The appeal court, however, found nothing unconstitutional about section 251 of the Criminal Code and, in fact, ruled that guarantees of life, liberty and security of person don't apply to abortion. Further, at the original jury trial, the doctors had argued that they had to perform abortions in order to protect women from the threat delays might represent to their life and health — a "defence of necessity", as the argument was known. The appeal court, however, criticized the trial judge for having let the jury consider the "misconceived" defence of necessity and said that, far from being impelled by urgency, the doctors had carefully mapped out their "conspiracy" to procure abortions illegally.

That was the rather precarious legal situation when Morgentaler and his associates appealed to the Supreme Court of Canada in early October 1986.

The Supreme Court of Canada in the 1980's

The seven men and two women who currently constitute Canada's Supreme Court are among the most powerful but least-known public figures in the country. Housed in a symmetrical four-storey granite structure in Ottawa, just west of the Parliament Buildings, for more than a century the role of the Court was to apply the law as defined by statute or legal precedent to the cases that came before it.

However, the seven judges hearing the Morgentaler case — Chief Justice Brian Dickson, and Justices Willard Estey, William McIntyre, Gerard La Forest, Jean Beetz, Antonio Lamer, and Bertha Wilson — enjoyed a considerably wider mandate than many of their predecessors. (Two justices — Gerald Le Dain and Claire L'Heureux-Dube, who was not appointed to the Court until the following year — did not participate in the case. Justice Estey has since retired.)

Much of the increased authority of the Court arose on April 17, 1982, when Queen Elizabeth II stood under a canopy on Parliament Hill, accompanied by dignitaries and television cameras, and proclaimed the Canadian

Constitution and its Charter of Rights and Freedoms as the supreme law of the land. With that proclamation, Canadian law and Canadian legislatures, including Parliament, were subordinated to the Constitution. In its new and expanded role, the Supreme Court now had the responsibility for interpreting the Constitution and the power to strike down laws that were in conflict with it.

Indeed, it was the constitutional question that was the centrepiece of the four dramatic days of hearing (October 7-10, 1986) held in the crowded walnut-paneled courtroom. Morgentaler's lawyer, Morris Manning, identified seven separate constitutional challenges to the 1969 abortion law, with particular emphasis on section 7 of the Charter, the clause providing for "life, liberty and security of the person". Although much of the evidence and argument during the presentation focused on such practical and factual matters as to whether the operation of the abortion law created situations of unequal access and dangerous delay, in the end both the Crown attorneys and the defence appeared to agree that it was the entirety of section 251 of the Criminal Code that must stand or fall, and not merely some portion of the mechanism, such as the legality of therapeutic abortion committees.

"It's an all-or-nothing situation?" asked Chief Justice Dickson at one point during Crown counsel Bonnie Wein's submission. "I think, my lord, in the end it is," she replied. Federal Justice Department lawyer Edward Sojonky used almost exactly the same words. "It is all or nothing," he told the seven judges. "Section 251 must remain as it is found in the Criminal Code or fall completely." With that, the Court retired to its chambers to begin the lengthy process of deliberation, writing and consultation that would eventuate in a decision — hopefully, one that would be upheld by a clear majority.

At this point, it's useful to note that the Court has wide latitude in making its decisions. It was not at all a foreordained conclusion as to what issues the Court would decide to make the basis of its judgment. Of course, the Court could — and there was increasing speculation in the legal community that it would — decide the constitutional question. But that was not its only option.

In the Morgentaler case, an appeal court had overturned a jury decision. It was possible that the Supreme Court might simply strike down the provision in the Criminal Code that allows judges who don't hear a trial to overrule an acquittal by juries who did, thus bringing Canadian law into line with that in Britain and the United States. If the Court merely overturned what was known as "judicial supremacy", it could then say that the remaining constitutional questions need not be answered because Morgentaler and his colleagues were now free. In fact, it was not uncommon practice, at least in decades past, for judges to answer the minimum necessary questions to dispose of the case before them.

Alternatively, the justices might decide for Morgentaler simply by finding that some portion of the mechanism provided by the abortion law was unfair, freeing the defendants and thus leaving Parliament to patch up an essentially unaltered law. Similarly, if the Court decided against Morgentaler, requiring the physician to be retried on the original charges before another jury, it could substantially affect future defence options by declaring whether or not, for example, to permit the defence of necessity used in previous trials.

While a unanimous decision would be preferable, in a case of such magnitude and complexity that was unlikely. Nonetheless, it was hoped that the lengthy deliberations would produce a clear majority rather than an ambiguous outcome. As University of Toronto law professor Bernard Dickens, an abortion law expert, commented, "To end up with a 4-3 split on such a fundamental issue would leave us nowhere and make the Court look bad." In any case, even a clear decision would likely produce several different opinions as various justices, while concurring on the main points, emphasized different reasons.

In fact, several of the justices were at work on written reasons. Chief Justice Dickson, the 71-year-old former Winnipeg lawyer and Manitoba judge who had been appointed in April 1984 to succeed former Chief Justice Bora Laskin, could be expected to offer the lead. His views would be supported by Justice Lamer. As well, Justice Jean Beetz, with the concurrence of Justice Estey, was working on an opinion that concentrated on the procedural requirements of the law. Justice Bertha Wilson, 64, a former Toronto lawyer and Ontario appellate judge who in March 1982 became the first woman appointed to the Supreme Court, was also preparing an opinion, one that promised to be widely read. Finally, Justice William McIntyre, 69, a former judge on the B.C. Court of Appeal who had served on the Supreme Court since 1979, was drafting, with the concurrence of Justice La Forest, what would turn out to be a dissenting opinion.

Decision on Abortion

When Morgentaler went to Ottawa on January 28, 1988 to receive the decision, the staff members of his Toronto clinic, and supporters throughout the country, were as much braced for defeat as they were hoping for victory. Co-defendant Robert Scott was reportedly so pessimistic about the outcome that he didn't want to spend the money to fly to Ottawa from Toronto to hear the ruling. Various commentators noted that Morgentaler's lawyer, Morris Manning, had faced an uphill battle which would require the Supreme Court to overturn a unanimous ruling by the widely respected judges of Ontario's Court of Appeal if Morgentaler was to win. Thus, the physician entering the colonnaded facade of the Supreme Court building had little cause to be confident of a favourable outcome that morning.

There was no ambiguity in the Supreme Court's decision. In a decisive 5-2 ruling, the Court declared that Canada's abortion law was unconstitutional because it violated a woman's right to "life, liberty and security of the person". As the stark front-page headline in the Toronto *Globe and Mail* trumpeted the next morning: "Abortion law scrapped." Its subhead, "Women get free choice", was, however, premature. The decision wiped the abortion law off the books and, in the process, freed Morgentaler and his colleagues.

Since co-editor Shelagh Day provides an extended interpretation of the meaning of the decision on abortion, only a brief summary of its contents is required here. In its boldest Charter case decision to date, the Court indicated unequivocally that it was prepared to use the Charter of Rights and Freedoms. Chief Justice Dickson's language was both tough and forthright. "State interference with bodily integrity and serious state-imposed psychological stress, at least in the criminal law context, constitutes a breach of security of the person," he declared. "Section 251 [of the Criminal Code] clearly interferes with a woman's physical integrity. Forcing a woman, by threat of criminal sanction, to carry a foetus to term unless she meets certain criteria unrelated to her own priorities and aspirations, is a profound interference with a woman's body and thus an infringement of security of the person."

Justice Bertha Wilson was no less unambiguous about what was at stake. "Section 251 of the Criminal Code, which limits the pregnant woman's access to abortion, violates her right to life, liberty and security of the person within the meaning of section 7 of the Charter in a way that does not accord with the principles of fundamental justice," Wilson said.

"The right to liberty contained in section 7," she continued, "guarantees to every individual a degree of personal autonomy over important decisions intimately affecting his or her private life. Liberty in a free and democratic society does not require the state to approve such decisions, but it does require the state to respect them. A woman's decision to terminate her pregnancy falls within this class of protected decisions. It is one that will have profound psychological, economic and social consequences for her. It is a decision that deeply reflects the way a woman thinks about herself and her relationship to others and to society at large. It is not just a medical decision; it is a profound social and ethical one as well." There was little mistaking the import of Wilson's ringing prose. "The decision whether or not to terminate a pregnancy," she added, "is essentially a moral decision and in a free and democratic society the conscience of the individual must be paramount to that of the state."

In addition to these fundamental pronouncements, Dickson, Lamer, Beetz, Estey and Wilson all commented extensively on the workings of the abortion law they had struck down. As Chief Justice Dickson put it, "A second breach of the right to security of the person occurs independently as a result of the delay in obtaining therapeutic abortions caused by the mandatory procedures of section 251, which results in a higher probability of complications and greater risk. The harm to the psychological integrity of women seeking abortions also was clearly established."

The Court also offered some advice on the status of the foetus, although the question of formally determining whether or not it had constitutional standing wasn't before the Court. Justice Wilson saw the protection of the foetus as a "perfectly valid legislative objective", though she struck down section 251 as an instrument for accomplishing that goal. She suggested that "the foetus should be viewed in differential and developmental terms. This view of the foetus supports a permissive approach to abortion in the early stages where the woman's autonomy would be absolute and a restrictive approach in the later stages where the state's interest in protecting the foetus would justify its prescribing conditions." Wilson also offered a view on the appropriate venue for determining such conditions. "The precise point in the development of the foetus at which the state's interest in its protection becomes 'compelling' should be left to the informed judgment of the legislature, which is in a position to receive submissions on the subject from all the relevant disciplines."

For Henry Morgentaler, the Supreme Court decision on abortion was a thorough vindication "beyond my wildest dreams". As he emerged from the Ottawa courtroom that morning, hemmed in by a phalanx of police escorts and a mob of pressing reporters, Morgentaler declared, "Bravo for the Supreme Court of Canada. Bravo for the women of Canada. Justice for the women of Canada has finally arrived." Whether it had really arrived, and whether it would be equally distributed, however, was a matter to be determined in the ensuing days.

The Text

The simple premise of the publication of the Supreme Court of Canada decision on abortion in a popular form is our belief that the judgment merits a wider and more general audience than the legal community.

Readers who don't make a practice of thumbing through court decisions will be pleasantly surprised, we believe, to find the justices' opinions in the Morgentaler case both accessible and eminently readable. Accordingly, we offer here the complete text of the decision in the form in which it appeared, with minimal editing, so that it will be useful to those who have a professional interest in it and to provide general readers with the true flavour of legal reasoning. We also include, in addition to an interpretive essay, the Court's official summary of the judgment as an appendix.

Admittedly, at first sight, the "reasons for judgment", as these opinions are known, can appear a bit daunting. In short order, however, a seemingly mysterious phrase, such as "...Estey J. observed in *Law Society of Upper Canada v. Skapinker*, [1984] 1 S.C.R. 357 at 377..." self-evidently translates into "Justice Estey said, in a 1984 case involving the Law Society of Upper Canada and a person named Skapinker, a report of which can be found in such-and-such a volume of the Supreme Court Reports on page 377, the following..." Legal readers, familiar with this form of referencing, are thus enabled to rush off to their nearest legal library and locate the passage; general readers, presumably, will simply pass over this bit of shorthand.

Part of this frequent referral to previous decisions is explained by the fact that the courts are intended, almost by definition, to be a conservative institution. What's fascinating for the general reader first coming upon these judgments is to see first-hand how the justices "work" a piece of law, nodding to earlier interpretations and precedents, and yet attempting to come to terms with a changing societal sense of what is right in a particular instance.

What readers will find here is a series of closely reasoned arguments about several questions fundamental to Canadian life. As we've noted above, beyond the legal status of the abortion law, the Court has pertinent thoughts about the meaning of the highest law in the land, the 1982 Charter of Rights and Freedoms. The

Court is particularly concerned to give us a clearer idea of what is meant by the provision in section 7 of the Charter that guarantees Canadians "life, liberty and security of the person." Although the opinions of the justices, as we've noted, frequently refer to other cases and documents which are perhaps primarily of interest to people in the legal profession, those references don't pose an obstacle to the general reader. In each instance, the justices clearly spell out the point being made in citing previous case law.

The presentations of the justices have an internal logic which is relatively straightforward. The main thing to keep in mind is that the Court is examining a particular section of the Canadian Criminal Code. The section, 251, is the law on abortion passed by Parliament some two decades ago. As noted previously, it's a law that both makes abortion a crime and provides exceptions to the law that permit abortions to be carried out under certain specified circumstances. The exceptions provide a legal defence for persons who secure abortions under the permitted circumstances.

The primary question that the Supreme Court asked was: Does the abortion law violate the constitutional guarantee of "security of the person" provided by section 7 of the Charter of Rights and Freedoms? By a vote of 5-2, the justices said, yes, the security of the person of a woman seeking an abortion is violated by the Criminal Code abortion law. However, the full text of section 7 says, "Everyone has the right to life, liberty and security of the person and the right not to be deprived thereof except in accordance with the principles of fundamental justice." Therefore, the Court then asks, given that the abortion law violates the security of the person guarantee, does that deprivation of rights occur in accordance with the principles of fundamental justice? The Morgentaler judgment decides that, no, the deprivation of rights doesn't accord with the principles of fundamental justice and, therefore, cannot be permitted.

However, the Constitution provides another out in certain exceptional circumstances. The very first section of the Charter says that the rights and freedoms set out in it are "subject only to such reasonable limits prescribed by law as can be demonstrably justified in a free and democratic society." The Court then turns to section 1 and asks, given that the abortion law violates section 7 of the Charter, is it nonetheless a "reasonable limit" that can be "justified in a free and democratic society"? That is, can the abortion law be "saved" by section 1? Again, by a vote of 5-2, the Court decided, no, it was not reasonable under the terms of section 1 of the Charter for the abortion law to override the "security of the person" provision in section 7 of the Charter. Thus, the Criminal Code abortion law was struck down.

In assessing the constitutional issue, the Court was also interested in the workings of the abortion law itself. The justices wanted to determine if it was fair. That is, the law provides a defence against the crime of abortion. Was that defence real or was it merely illusory? Did the complicated mechanism laid out in the abortion law work in such a way that it presented unreasonable obstacles to women seeking abortions? In both instances, the majority of the Court judged that the law was seriously flawed.

Finally, the Court addresses several lesser, more technical matters of law. They range from the rights of appeal courts to review jury verdicts to the propriety of a lawyer suggesting that a jury can ignore certain laws on occasion. Although subsidiary to the major questions in this case, they are not without interest, even to general readers.

Though the Morgentaler decision is unquestionably of landmark stature, nonetheless the Court is consciously cautious to avoid a definitive interpretation of the Constitution — even of section 7. The 1982 Constitution Act is but a few years old, and it's clear that the Court sees its own enlarged role as gradualist. As Chief Justice Dickson remarks, "I do not think it would be appropriate to attempt an all-encompassing explication of so important a provision as section 7 so early in the history of Charter interpretation. The Court should be presented with a wide variety of claims and factual situations before articulating the full range of section 7 rights." With that in mind, we believe that the interpretation of section 7 offered is of substantial interest.

The Immediate Aftermath

Even as Dr. Morgentaler was leaving the Supreme Court on the morning of January 28, 1988, two crowds began gathering in below-zero temperatures outside Morgentaler's Harbord Street clinic in Toronto. Around the entrance of the long-embattled clinic, pro-choice supporters chanted their approval of the Court decision; across the street, kept separate by police, anti-abortion demonstrators voiced their continued opposition. It was but the most tangible sign of the renewal of a debate that in the next few weeks would dominate the public forum.

Before the week was out, various provincial governments were responding to the decision by announcing a patchwork of policies providing differing degrees of accessibility to abortion, and Justice Minister Ramon Hnatyshyn, on behalf of the federal government, promised "to provide the leadership that is required on this issue".

The following Monday, Ontario Health Minister Elinor Caplan, having already dismantled the therapeutic abortion committees found offensive in the Supreme Court judgment, announced that the Ontario government would pay for all abortions done in the province, including those performed in clinics or doctors' offices. The decision made Ontario the second province, after Quebec, to cover the costs of such operations.

Throughout the country, the provinces, which administer Canada's universal medical care programs, adopted sharply different policies. By mid-February, two weeks after the Court's decision, they ranged from relatively accessible services available in Quebec, Ontario and Manitoba to the complete absence of available services in Prince Edward Island. Other jurisdictions simply muddled along, some refusing to condone the idea of free-standing abortion clinics, others attempting to develop systems requiring physicians to provide a "second opinion" authorizing the procedure.

Perhaps the most extreme reaction came from the British Columbia government of Premier Bill Vander Zalm. On February 10, 1988, the provincial cabinet decided to refuse public financing of abortions. In an unusual move, the B.C. cabinet passed regulations to the provincial Medical Services Act declaring that abortions would not be considered medically required unless a woman's life was in danger. Not even pregnancies resulting from rape or incest would qualify, insisted Vander Zalm.

Within a week, the B.C. Civil Liberties Association was before the provincial Supreme Court, asking it to strike down the policy on the grounds that the cabinet didn't have the right to withhold medical services from women and, further, that the B.C. government was bound by its own provincial laws to provide a full range of health services. The civil liberties group consciously avoided a full-scale and inevitably lengthy constitutional challenge to the policy and instead contented itself with a narrower administrative law case in the hope of securing immediate relief from what had become a chaotic situation for women seeking abortions.

On March 7, 1988, B.C. Supreme Court Chief Justice Allan McEachern, in the first legal ruling since the Supreme Court of Canada's decision, swiftly and unequivocally struck down Vander Zalm's anti-abortion policy. Said Judge McEachern: "Such a determination, that abortion services are not medically required, purports to remove services that are in fact medically required from the definition of insured service. Such a regulation is invalid, being one that is not authorized by the statute and is inconsistent with the statute and with common sense," ruled McEachern in plain-spoken language that admitted of no doubts as to the meaning of his decision.

Indeed, the province's attorney-general, Brian Smith, speaking for the government, was inclined to prompt obedience. "I read the decision this way:" said Mr. Smith. "It not only says that to de-insure abortion from the Medical Services Act is flawed, but there's a strong suggestion that if we were to re-enact it, or to do it another way, we would fail under the Charter." B.C.'s top legal officer said he would advise his government to neither appeal the decision or re-enact the law. "We have to respect the law. The law today is that our regulation is not valid," said Smith, bringing a momentary calm to a particularly turbulent situation.

What B.C. Chief Justice McEachern's decision pointed up was a glaring and recurrent anomaly in Canada's federalist system, which divides powers between the federal and provincial governments. If there is a national, universal medical system guaranteeing equal services and access to all Canadians, and if that system is administered at the provincial level, isn't it likely, when it comes to a controversial issue such as abortion, that the result of provincial decision-making will be an inconsistent and unfair patchwork of different policies that substantially departs from the original intentions of having a national medical policy providing equal benefits? Presumably, that's what was on Judge McEachern's mind when he wrote, "It is apparent that Parliament must resolve this profound agony between competing rights and interests." By spring 1988, the focus of deliberation had largely returned to the Canadian Parliament, the forum where it would be decided whether or not new legislation was necessary in light of the Supreme Court of Canada's decision on abortion.

Acknowledgments

Since the foregoing account is largely dependent on contemporaneous reportage, the editors wish to acknowledge their debt to the working press in making our version of events possible. The Toronto *Globe and Mail*'s Kirk Makin has provided consistently reliable coverage of legal matters for a number of years; we have also benefited from the reporting of Ann Rauhala and John Cruickshank of the same publication, as well as an essay by Lynn Lathrop, spokeswoman for the Ontario Coalition for Abortion Clinics, published in the February 2, 1988 edition of the *Globe*. In addition, we have relied on the January 11 and February 8, 1988 editions of *Maclean's* magazine, and tender our thanks to reporters Mary Janigan, Chris Wood and Rae Corelli of that journal, and to Anne Collins, whose essay "An Unambiguous Call From The Court" appeared in the newsmagazine's pages.

Finally, we wish to thank B.C. Civil Liberties Association president John Dixon, University of British Columbia law professor and BCCLA board member Phil Bryden, and Lynn Smith, who is a representative of the Women's Legal Education and Action Fund, as well as a UBC law professor and BCCLA board member, for much helpful advice on these matters. Equally, we are grateful to Gwen Brodsky, Anita Braha, and Margaret

Day for their comments and suggestions. Responsibility for errors of fact and interpretation of course rests with the editors.

Readers interested in recent and more extended discussions of abortion and the court are referred to Arlene Tigar McLaren and Angus McLaren, *The Bedroom and the State: The Changing Practices and Politics of Abortion and Contraception in Canada* (McClelland and Stewart, 1987), and Peter H. Russell, *The Judiciary in Canada: The Third Branch of Government* (McGraw-Hill Ryerson, 1987).

Stan Persky
Vancouver, B.C.
May, 1988

Supreme Court of Canada

DR. HENRY MORGENTALER
DR. LESLIE FRANK SMOLING
DR. ROBERT SCOTT

v.

HER MAJESTY THE QUEEN
and
THE ATTORNEY GENERAL OF CANADA

CORAM:
The Rt. Hon. Brian Dickson, P.C.
The Hon. Mr. Justice Beetz
The Hon. Mr. Justice Estey
The Hon. Mr. Justice McIntyre
The Hon. Mr. Justice Lamer
The Hon. Mme Justice Wilson
The Hon. Mr. Justice La Forest

Appeal Heard: October 7, 8, 9, 10, 1986
Judgment Rendered: January 28, 1988
Reasons for Judgment by: The Rt. Hon. Brian
   Dickson, P.C.
Concurred in by: The Hon. Mr. Justice Lamer
Reasons for Judgment by: The Hon. Mr. Justice Beetz
Concurred in by: The Hon. Mr. Justice Estey
Reasons for Judgment by: The Hon. Mme Justice
   Wilson
Dissenting Reasons by: The Hon. Mr. Justice
   McIntyre
Concurred in by: The Hon. Mr. Justice La Forest

Reasons for Judgment: Chief Justice Brian Dickson

Concurred in by
  Justice Antonio Lamer

The principal issue raised by this appeal is whether the abortion provisions of the Criminal Code infringe the "right to life, liberty and security of the person and the right not to be deprived thereof except in accordance with the principles of fundamental justice" as formulated in s. 7 of the Canadian Charter of Rights and Freedoms. The appellants, Dr. Henry Morgentaler, Dr. Leslie Frank Smoling and Dr. Robert Scott, have raised thirteen distinct grounds of appeal. During oral submissions, however, it became apparent that the primary focus of the case was upon the s. 7 argument. It is submitted by the appellants that s. 251 of the Criminal Code, R.S.C. 1970, c. C-34, contravenes s. 7 of the Canadian Charter of Rights and Freedoms and that s. 251 should be struck down. Counsel for the Crown admitted during the course of her submissions that s. 7 of the Charter was indeed "the key" to the entire appeal. As for the remaining ground of appeal, only a few brief comments are necessary. First of all, I agree with the disposition made by the Court of Appeal of the non-Charter issues, many of which have already been adequately dealt with in earlier cases by this Court. I am also of the view that the arguments concerning the alleged invalidity of s. 605 under ss. 7 and 11 of the Charter are unfounded. In view of my resolution of the s. 7 issue, it will not be necessary for me to address the appellants' other Charter arguments and I expressly refrain from commenting upon their merits.

During argument before this Court, counsel for the Crown emphasized repeatedly that it is not the role of the judiciary in Canada to evaluate the wisdom of legislation enacted by our democratically elected representatives, or to second-guess difficult policy choices that confront all governments. In *Morgentaler v. The Queen*, [1976] 1 S.C.R. 616, at p. 671, [hereinafter *Morgentaler (1975)*] I stressed that the Court had "not been called upon to decide, or even to enter, the loud and continuous public debate on abortion." Eleven years later, the controversy persists, and it remains true that this Court cannot presume to resolve all of the competing claims advanced in vigorous and healthy public debate. Courts and legislators in other democratic societies have reached completely contradictory decisions when asked to weigh the competing values relevant to the abortion question. See, e.g., *Roe v. Wade*, 410 U.S. 113 (1973); *Paton v. United Kingdom* (1980), 3 E.H.R.R. (European Court of Human Rights); *The Abortion Decision of the Federal Constitutional Court - First Senate - of the Federal Republic of Germany*, February 25, 1975, translated and reprinted in (1976), 9 John Marshall J. Prac. and Proc. 605; and the Abortion Act 1967, 1967, c. 87 (U.K.).

But since 1975, and the first *Morgentaler* decision, the Court has been given added responsibilities. I stated in *Morgentaler (1975)*, at p. 671, that

> The values we must accept for the purposes of this appeal are those expressed by Parliament which holds the view that the desire of a woman to be relieved of her pregnancy is not, of itself, justification for performing an abortion.

Although no doubt it is still fair to say that courts are not the appropriate forum for articulating complex and controversial programmes of public policy, Canadian courts are now charged with the crucial obligation of ensuring that the legislative initiatives pursued by our Parliament and legislatures conform to the democratic values expressed in the Canadian Charter of Rights and Freedoms. As Justice McIntyre states in his reasons for judgment, ". . . the task of the Court in this case is not to solve nor seek to solve what might be called the abortion issue, but simply to measure the content of s. 251 against the Charter." It is in this latter sense that the current Morgentaler appeal differs from the one we heard a decade ago.

I.

The Court stated the following constitutional questions:
1. Does s. 251 of the Criminal Code of Canada infringe or deny the rights and freedoms guaranteed by ss. 2(a), 7, 12, 15, 27 and 28 of the Canadian Charter of Rights and Freedoms?
2. If s. 251 of the Criminal Code of Canada infringes or denies the rights and freedoms guaranteed by ss. 2(a), 7, 12, 15, 27 and 28 of the Canadian Charter of Rights and Freedoms, is s. 251 justified by s. 1 of the Canadian Charter of Rights and Freedoms and therefore not inconsistent with the Constitution Act, 1982?
3. Is s. 251 of the Criminal Code of Canada *ultra vires* the Parliament of Canada?

4. Does s. 251 of the Criminal Code of Canada violate s. 96 of the Constitution Act, 1867?

5. Does s. 251 of the Criminal Code of Canada unlawfully delegate federal criminal power to provincial Ministers of Health or Therapeutic Abortion Committees, and in doing so, has the Federal Government abdicated its authority in this area?

6. Do ss. 605 and 610(3) of the Criminal Code of Canada infringe or deny the rights and freedoms guaranteed by ss. 7, 11(d), 11(f), 11(h) and 24(1) of the Canadian Charter of Rights and Freedoms?

7. If ss. 605 and 610(3) of the Criminal Code of Canada infringe or deny the rights and freedoms guaranteed by ss. 7, 11(d), 11(f), 11(h) and 24(1) of the Canadian Charter of Rights and Freedoms, are ss. 605 and 610(3) justified by s. 1 of the Canadian Charter of Rights and Freedoms and therefore not inconsistent with the Constitution Act, 1982?

The Attorney General of Canada intervened to support the respondent Crown.

II. Relevant Statutory and Constitutional Provisions

The Criminal Code

251 (1) Every one who, with intent to procure the miscarriage of a female person, whether or not she is pregnant, uses any means for the purpose of carrying out his intention is guilty of an indictable offence and is liable to imprisonment for life.

(2) Every female person who, being pregnant, with intent to procure her own miscarriage, uses any means or permits any means to be used for the purpose of carrying out her intention is guilty of an indictable offence and is liable to imprisonment for two years.

(3) In this section, "means" include

(a) the administration of a drug or other noxious thing,

(b) the use of an instrument, and

(c) manipulation of any kind.

(4) Subsections (1) and (2) do not apply to

(a) a qualified medical practitioner, other than a member of a therapeutic abortion committee for any hospital, who in good faith uses in an accredited or approved hospital any means for the purpose of carrying out his intention to procure the miscarriage of a female person, or

(b) a female person who, being pregnant, permits a qualified medical practioner to use in an accredited or approved hospital any means described in paragraph (a) for the purpose of carrying out her intention to procure her own miscarriage, if, before the use of those means, the therapeutic abortion committee for that accredited or approved hospital, by a majority of the members of the committee and at a meeting of the committee at which the case of such female person has been reviewed,

(c) has by certificate in writing stated that in its opinion the continuation of the pregnancy of such female person would or would be likely to endanger her life or health, and

(d) has caused a copy of such certificate to be given to the qualified medical practitioner.

(5) The Minister of Health of a province may by order

(a) require a therapeutic abortion committee for any hospital in that province, or any member thereof, to furnish to him a copy of any certificate described in paragraph (4)(c) issued, by that committee, together with such other information relating to the circumstances surrounding the issue of that certificate as he may require, or

(b) require a medical practitioner who, in that

province, has procured the miscarriage of any female person named in a certificate described in paragraph (4)(*c*), to furnish to him a copy of that certificate, together with such other information relating to the procuring of the miscarriage as he may require.

(6) For the purposes of subsection (4) and (5) and this subsection

"accredited hospital" means a hospital accredited by the Canadian Council on Hospital Accreditation in which diagnostic services and medical, surgical and obstetrical treatment are provided;

"approved hospital" means a hospital in a province approved for the purposes of this section by the Minister of Health of that province;

"board" means the board of governors, management or directors, or the trustees, commission or other person or group of persons having the control and management of an accredited or approved hospital;

"Minister of Health" means

(*a*) in the Provinces of Ontario, Quebec, New Brunswick, Manitoba, Newfoundland and Prince Edward Island, the Minister of Health,

(*a*.1) in the Province of Alberta, the Minister of Hospitals and Medical Care,

(*b*) in the Province of British Columbia, the Minister of Health Services and Hospital Insurance,

(*c*) in the Provinces of Nova Scotia and Saskatchewan, the Minister of Public Health, and

(*d*) in the Yukon Territory and the Northwest Territories, the Minister of National Health and Welfare;

"qualified medical practitioner" means a person

entitled to engage in the practice of medicine under the laws of the province in which the hospital referred to in subsection (4) is situated;

"therapeutic abortion committee" for any hospital means a committee comprised of not less than three members each of whom is a qualified medical practitioner, appointed by the board of that hospital for the purpose of considering and determining questions relating to terminations of pregnancy within the hospital.

(7) Nothing in subsection (4) shall be construed as making unnecessary the obtaining of any authorization or consent that is or may be required, otherwise than under this Act, before any means are used for the purpose of carrying out an intention to procure the miscarriage of a female person.

The Canadian Charter of Rights and Freedoms

1. The Canadian Charter of Rights and Freedoms guarantees the rights and freedoms set out in it subject only to such reasonable limits prescribed by law as can be demonstrably justified in a free and democratic society. . . .

7. Everyone has the right to life, liberty and security of the person and the right not be deprived thereof except in accordance with the principles of fundamental justice.

III. Procedural History

The three appellants are all duly qualified medical practitioners who together set up a clinic in Toronto to perform abortions upon women who had not obtained a certificate from a therapeutic abortion committee of an accredited or approved hospital as required by s. 251(4). The doctors had made public statements questioning the wisdom of the abortion laws in Canada and asserting that a woman has an unfettered right to choose whether or not an abortion is appropriate in her individual circumstances.

Indictments were preferred against the appellants charging that they conspired with each other between November 1982 and July 1983 with intent to procure the miscarriage of female persons, using an induced suction technique to carry out that intent, contrary to s. 423(1)(d) and s. 251(1) of the Criminal Code.

Counsel for the appellants moved to quash the indictment or to stay the proceedings before pleas were entered on the grounds that s. 251 of the Criminal Code was *ultra vires* the Parliament of Canada, infringed ss. 2(a), 7 and 12 of the Charter, and was inconsistent with s. 1(b) of the Canadian Bill of Rights. The trial judge, Parker A.C.J.H.C., dismissed the motion, and an appeal to the Ontario Court of Appeal was dismissed. The trial proceeded before Parker A.C.J.H.C. and a jury, and the three accused were acquitted. The Crown appealed the acquittal to the Court of Appeal and the appellants filed a cross-appeal. The Court of Appeal allowed the appeal, set aside the verdict of acquittal and ordered a new trial. The Court held that the cross-appeal related to issues already raised in the appeal, and the issues were therefore examined as part of the appeal. Leave to appeal was granted by this Court.

IV. Section 7 of the Charter

In his submissions, counsel for the appellants argued that the Court should recognize a very wide ambit for the rights protected under s. 7 of the Charter. Basing his argument largely on American constitutional theories and authorities, Mr. Manning submitted that the right to "life, liberty and security of the person" is a wide-ranging right to control one's own life and to promote one's individual autonomy. The right would therefore include a right to privacy and a right to make unfettered decisions about one's own life.

In my opinion, it is neither necessary nor wise in this appeal to explore the broadest implications of s. 7 as counsel would wish us to do. I prefer to rest my conclusions on a narrower analysis than that put forward on behalf of the appellants. I do not think it would be appropriate to attempt an all-encompassing explication of so important a provision as s. 7 so early in the history of Charter interpretation. The Court should be presented with a wide variety of claims and factual situations before articulating the full range of s. 7 rights. I will therefore limit my comments to some interpretive principles already set down by the Court and to an analysis of only two aspects of s. 7, the right to "security of the person" and "the principles of fundamental justice".

A. Interpreting Section 7

The goal of Charter interpretation is to secure for all people "the full benefit of the Charter's protection": *R. v. Big M Drug Mart Ltd.*, [1985] 1 S.C.R. 295, at p. 344. To attain that goal, this Court has held consistently that the proper technique for the interpretation of Charter provisions is to pursue a "purposive" analysis of the right guaranteed. A right recognized in the Charter is "to be understood, in other words, in the light of the interests it was meant to protect": *R. v. Big M Drug Mart Ltd.*, at p. 344. (See also *Hunter v. Southam Inc.*, [1984] 2 S.C.R. 145; and *R. v. Therens*, [1985] 1 S.C.R. 613.)

In *Singh v. Minister of Employment and Immigration*, [1985] 1 S.C.R. 177, at p. 204, Justice Wilson

emphasized that there are three distinct elements to the
s. 7 right, that "life, liberty, and security of the person"
are independent interests, each of which must be given
independent significance by the Court (p. 205). This
interpretation was adopted by a majority of the Court,
per Lamer J., in *Re B.C. Motor Vehicle Act*, [1985] 2
S.C.R. 486, at p. 500. It is therefore possible to treat
only one aspect of the first part of s. 7 before determining whether any infringement of that interest accords
with the principles of fundamental justice. (See *Singh*,
Re B.C. Motor Vehicle Act, and *R. v. Jones*, [1986] 2
S.C.R. 284.)

With respect to the second part of s. 7, in early academic commentary one of the principal concerns was
whether the reference to "principles of fundamental
justice" enables the courts to review the substance of
legislation. (See, e.g., Whyte, "Fundamental Justice:
The Scope and Application of Section 7 of the Charter"
in Canadian Institute for the Administration of Justice,
The Canadian Charter of Rights and Freedoms (n.d.);
and Garant, "Fundamental Freedoms and Natural Justice" in W. Tarnopolsky and G.-A Beaudoin, *The Canadian Charter of Rights and Freedoms: Commentary*
(1982)). In *Re B.C. Motor Vehicle Act*, Lamer J. noted
at p. 497 that any attempt to draw a sharp line between
procedure and substance would be ill-conceived. He
suggested further that it would not be beneficial in Canada to allow a debate which is rooted in United States
constitutional dilemmas to shape our interpretation of s.
7 (p. 498):

> We would, in my view, do our own Constitution a
> disservice to simply allow the American debate to de-
> fine the issue for us, all the while ignoring the truly
> fundamental structural differences between the two
> constitutions.

Lamer J. went on to hold that the principles of funda-

mental justice referred to in s. 7 can relate both to procedure and to substance, depending upon the circumstances presented before the Court.

I have no doubt that s. 7 does impose upon courts the
duty to review the substance of legislation once it has
been determined that the legislation infringes an individual's right to "life, liberty and security of the person." The section states clearly that those interests may
only be impaired if the principles of fundamental justice
are respected. Lamer J. emphasized, however, that the
courts should avoid "adjudication of the merits of public
policy" (p. 499). In the present case, I do not believe that
it is necessary for the Court to tread the fine line between
substantive review and the adjudication of public
policy. As in the *Singh* case, it will be sufficient to
investigate whether or not the impugned legislative
provisions meet the procedural standards of fundamental justice. First it is necessary to determine whether s.
251 of the Criminal Code impairs the security of the
person.

B. Security of the Person

The law has long recognized that the human body ought
to be protected from interference by others. At common
law, for example, any medical procedure carried out on
a person without that person's consent is an assault.
Only in emergency circumstances does the law allow
others to make decisions of this nature. Similarly, art.
19 of the Civil Code of Lower Canada provides that
"[t]he human person is inviolable" and that "[n]o person
may cause harm to the person of another without his
consent or without being authorized by law to do so".
"Security of the person", in other words, is not a value
alien to our legal landscape. With the advent of the
Charter, security of the person has been elevated to the
status of a constitutional norm. This is not to say that the

various forms of protection accorded to the human body by the common and civil law occupy a similar status. "Security of the person" must be given content in a manner sensitive to its constitutional position. The above examples are simply illustrative of our respect for individual physical integrity. (See Macdonald, "Procedural Due Process in Canadian Constitutional Law", 39 *U. Fla. L. Rev.* 217 (1987), at p. 248.) Nor is it to say that the state can never impair personal security interests. There may well be valid reasons for interfering with security of the person. It is to say, however, that if the state does interfere with security of the person, the Charter requires such interference to conform with the principles of fundamental justice.

The appellants submitted that the "security of the person" protected by the Charter is an explicit right to control one's body and to make fundamental decisions about one's life. The Crown contended that "security of the person" is a more circumscribed interest and that, like all of the elements of s. 7, it at most relates to the concept of physical control, simply protecting the individual's interest in his or bodily integrity.

Canadian courts have already had occasion to address the scope of the interest protected under the rubric of "security of the person". In *R. v. Caddedu* (1982), 40 O.R. (2d) 128 (H.C.), at p. 139, the Ontario High Court emphasized that the right to security of the person, like each aspect of s. 7, is a basic right, the deprivation of which has severe consequences for an individual. This characterization was approved by this Court in *Re B.C. Motor Vehicle Act*, at p. 501. The Ontario Court of Appeal has held that the right to life, liberty and security of the person "would appear to relate to one's physical or mental integrity and one's control over these . . ." (*R. v. Videoflicks Ltd.* (1984), 48 O.R. (2d) 395, at p. 433 (C.A.)).

That conclusion is consonant with the holding of Jus-

tice Lamer in *Mills v. The Queen* [1986] 1 S.C.R. 863.
In *Mills*, Lamer J. was the only judge of this Court to
treat the right to security of the person in any detail.
Although the right arose in the context of s. 11(*b*) of the
Charter, Lamer J. stressed the close connection between the specific rights in ss. 8 to 14 and the more
generally applicable rights expressed in s. 7. Lamer J.
held, at pp. 919-20, that even in the specific context of
s. 11(*b*):

> . . . security of the person is not restricted to physical
> integrity; rather, it encompasses protection against
> "overlong subjection to vexations and vicissitudes of a
> pending criminal accusation". . . . These include stig-
> matization of the accused, loss of privacy, stress and
> anxiety resulting from a multitude of factors, including
> possible disruption of family, social life and work,
> legal costs, uncertainty as to the outcome and sanction.

If state-imposed psychological trauma infringes security of the person in the rather circumscribed case of s.
11(*b*), it should be relevant to the general case of s. 7
where the right is expressed in broader terms. (See
Whyte, p. 39.)

I note also that the Court has held in other contexts
that the psychological effect of state action is relevant in
assessing whether or not a Charter right has been
infringed. In *R. v. Therens*, at p. 644, Le Dain J. held
that "the element of psychological compulsion, in the
form of a reasonable perception of suspension of freedom of choice, is enough to make the restraint of liberty
involuntary" for the purposes of defining "detention" in
s. 10 of the Charter. A majority of the Court accepted the
conclusions of Le Dain J. on this issue.

It may well be that constitutional protection of the
above interests is specific to, and is only triggered by,
the invocation of our system of criminal justice. It must
not be forgotten, however, that s. 251 of the Code,
subject to subsection (4), makes it an indictable offence

for a person to procure the miscarriage and provides a maximum sentence of two years in the case of the woman herself, and a maximum sentence of life imprisonment in the case of another person. Like Justice Beetz, I do not find it necessary to decide how s. 7 would apply in other cases.

The case law leads me to the conclusion that state interference with bodily integrity and serious state-imposed psychological stress, at least in the criminal law context, constitute a breach of security of the person. It is not necessary in this case to determine whether the right extends further, to protect either interests central to personal autonomy, such as a right to privacy, or interests unrelated to criminal justice.

I wish to reiterate that finding a violation of security of the person does not end the s. 7 inquiry. Parliament could choose to infringe security of the person if it did so in a manner consistent with the principles of fundamental justice. The present discussion should therefore be seen as a threshold inquiry and the conclusions do not dispose definitively of all the issues relevant to s. 7. With that caution, I have no difficulty in concluding that the encyclopedic factual submissions addressed to us by counsel in the present appeal establish beyond any doubt that s. 251 of the Criminal Code is *prima facie* a violation of the security of the person of thousands of Canadian women who have made the difficult decision that they do not wish to continue with a pregnancy.

At the most basic physical and emotional level, every pregnant woman is told by the section that she cannot submit to a generally safe medical procedure that might be of clear benefit to her unless she meets criteria entirely unrelated to her own priorities and aspirations. Not only does the removal of decision making power threaten women in a physical sense; the indecision of knowing whether an abortion will be granted inflicts emotional stress. Section 251 clearly interferes with a woman's bodily integrity in both a physical and emotional sense. Forcing a woman, by threat of criminal sanction, to carry a foetus to term unless she meets certain criteria unrelated to her own priorities and aspirations, is a profound interference with a woman's body and thus a violation of security of the person. Section 251, therefore, is required by the Charter to comport with the principles of fundamental justice.

Although this interference with physical and emotional integrity is sufficient in itself to trigger a review of s. 251 against the principles of fundamental justice, the operation of the decision making mechanism set out in s. 251 creates additional glaring breaches of security of the person. The evidence indicates that s. 251 causes a certain amount of delay for women who are successful in meeting its criteria. In the context of abortion, any unnecessary delay can have profound consequences on the woman's physical and emotional well-being.

More specifically, in 1977, the *Report of the Committee on the Operation of the Abortion Law* (the *Badgley Report*) revealed that the average delay between a pregnant woman's first contact with a physician and a subsequent therapeutic abortion was eight weeks (p. 146). Although the situation appears to have improved since 1977, the extent of the improvement is not clear. The intervener, the Attorney General of Canada, submitted that the average delay in Ontario between the first visit to a physician and a therapeutic abortion was now between one and three weeks. Yet the respondent Crown admitted in a supplementary factum filed on November 27, 1986 with the permission of the Court that (p. 3):

the evidence discloses that some women may find it very difficult to obtain an abortion: by necessity, abortion services are limited, since hospitals have budgetary, time, space and staff constraints as well as many medical responsibilities. As a result of these problems a woman may have to apply to several hospitals.

If forced to apply to several different therapeutic abortion committees, there can be no doubt that a woman will experience serious delay in obtaining a therapeutic abortion. In her *Report on Therapeutic Abortion Services in Ontario* (the *Powell Report*), Dr. Marion Powell emphasized that (p. 7):

> The entire process [of obtaining an abortion] was found to be protracted with women requiring three to seven contacts with health professionals...

Revealing the full extent of this problem, Dr. Augustin Roy, the President of the Corporation Professionelle de Médecins du Québec, testified that studies showed that in Quebec the waiting time for a therapeutic abortion in hospital varied between one and six weeks.

These periods of delay may not seem unduly long, but in the case of abortion, the implications of any delay, according to the evidence, are potentially devastating. The first factor to consider is that different medical techniques are employed to perform abortions at different stages of pregnancy. The testimony of expert doctors at trial indicated that in the first twelve weeks of pregnancy, the relatively safe and simple suction dilation and curettage method of abortion is typically used in North America. From the thirteenth to the sixteenth week, the more dangerous dilation and evacuation procedure is performed, although much less often in Canada than in the United States. From the sixteenth week of pregnancy, the instillation method is commonly employed in Canada. This method requires the intra-amniotic introduction of prostoglandin, urea, or a saline solution, which causes a woman to go into labour, giving birth to a foetus which is usually dead, but not invariably so. The uncontroverted evidence showed that each method of abortion progressively increases risks to the woman. (See, e.g., Tyler, *et al.*, "Second Trimester Induced Abortion in the United States", Cases on Appeal, Vol. XXII, at p. 4601).

The second consideration is that even within the periods appropriate to each method of abortion, the evidence indicated that the earlier the abortion was performed, the fewer the complications and the lower the risk of mortality. For example, a study emanating from the Centre for Disease Control in Atlanta confirmed that "D & E [dilation and evacuation] procedures performed at 13 to 15 weeks' gestation were nearly 3 times safer than those performed at 16 weeks or later". (Cates and Grimes, "Deaths from Second Trimester Abortion by Dilation and Evacuation: Causes, Prevention, Facilities" (1981), 58 *Obstetrics and Gynecology* 401, at p. 401. See also the *Powell Report*, at p. 36). The Court was advised that because of their perceptions of risk, Canadian doctors often refuse to use the dilation and evacuation procedure from the thirteenth to sixteenth weeks and instead wait until they consider it appropriate to use the instillation technique. Even more revealing were the overall mortality statistics evaluated by Drs. Cates and Grimes. They concluded from their study of the relevant data that:

Anything that contributes to delay in performing abortions increases the complication rates by 15 to 30%, and the chance of dying by 50% for each week of delay.

These statistics indicate clearly that even if the average delay caused by s. 251 *per arguendo* is of only a couple of weeks' duration, the effects upon any particular woman can be serious and, occasionally, fatal.

It is no doubt true that the overall complication and mortality rates for women who undergo abortions are very low, but the increasing risks caused by delay are so

clearly established that I have no difficulty in concluding that the delay in obtaining therapeutic abortions
caused by the mandatory procedures of s. 251 is an
infringement of the purely physical aspect of the individual's right to security of the person. I should stress
that the marked contrast between the relative speed with
which abortions can be obtained at the government-
sponsored community clinics in Quebec and in hospitals under the s. 251 procedure was established at trial.
The evidence indicated that at the government-
sponsored clinics in Quebec, the maximum delay was
less than a week. One must conclude, and perhaps un-
derline, that the delay experienced by many women
seeking a therapeutic abortion, be it of one, two, four, or
six weeks duration, is caused in large measure by the
requirements of s. 251 itself.

The above physical interference caused by the delays
created by s. 251, involving a clear risk of damage to the
physical well-being of a woman, is sufficient, in my
view, to warrant inquiring whether s. 251 comports
with the principles of fundamental justice. However,
there is yet another infringement of security of the person. It is clear from the evidence that s. 251 harms the
psychological integrity of women seeking abortions. A
1985 report of the Canadian Medical Association, discussed in the *Powell Report*, at p. 15, emphasized that
the procedure involved in s. 251, with the concomitant
delays, greatly increases the stress levels of patients and
that this can lead to more physical complications associated with abortion. A specialist in fertility control, Dr.
Henry David, was qualified as an expert witness at trial
on the psychological impact upon women of delay in the
process of obtaining an abortion. He testified that his
own studies had demonstrated that there is increased
psychological stress imposed upon women who are
forced to wait for abortions, and that this stress is
compounded by the uncertainty whether or not a thera-

peutic abortion committee will actually grant approval.

Perhaps the most powerful testimony regarding the psychological impact upon women caused by the delay inherent in s. 251 procedures was offered at trial by Dr. Jane Hodgson, the Medical Director of the Women's Health Center in Duluth, Minnesota. She was called to testify as to her experiences with Canadian women who had come to the Women's Health Center for abortions. Her testimony was extensive, but the flavour may be gleaned from the following short excerpts:

> May I add one other thing that I think is very vital, and that is that many of these [Canadian] women come down because they know they will be delayed in getting, first, permission, then delayed in getting a hospital bed, or getting into the hospital, and so they know they will have to have saline [instillation] procedures. And some of them have been through this, and others know what it is about, and they will do almost anything to avoid having a saline procedure.
>
> And of course, that is — I consider that a very cruel type of medical care and will do anything to help them avoid this type of treatment. . . .
>
> The cost, the time consumed, the medical risks, the mental anguish — all of this is cruelty, in this day and age, because it's [the instillation procedure] an obsolete procedure that is essentially disappearing in the United States.

I have already noted that the instillation procedure requires a woman actually to experience labour and to suffer through the birth of a foetus that is usually but not always dead. Statistics from 1982 indicated that 33.4 per cent of second trimester abortions in Ontario were done by instillation, and the *Powell Report* revealed, at p. 36, that even in 1986 there persisted a high incidence of second trimester abortions in Ontario. The psychological injury caused by delay in obtaining abortions, much of which must be attributed to the procedures set out in s. 251, constitutes an additional infringement of the right to security of the person.

In its supplementary factum and in oral submissions, the Crown argued that evidence of what could be termed "administrative inefficiency" is not relevant to the evaluation of legislation for the purposes of s. 7 of the Charter. The Crown argued that only evidence regarding the purpose of legislation is relevant. The assumption, of course, is that any impairment to the physical or psychological interests of individuals caused by s. 251 of the Criminal Code does not amount to an infringement of security of the person because the injury is caused by practical difficulties and is not intended by the legislator.

The submission is faulty on two counts. First, as a practical matter it is not possible in the case of s. 251 to erect a rigid barrier between the purposes of the section and the administrative procedures established to carry those purposes into effect. For example, although it may be true that Parliament did not enact s. 251 intending to create delays in obtaining therapeutic abortions, the evidence demonstrates that the system established by the section for obtaining a therapeutic abortion certificate inevitably does create significant delays. It is not possible to say that delay results only from administrative constraints, such as limited budgets or a lack of qualified persons to sit on therapeutic abortion committees. Delay results from the cumbersome operating requirements of s. 251 itself. (See, by way of analogy, *R. v. Therens*, *per* Le Dain J., at p. 645). Although the mandate given to the courts under the Charter does not, generally speaking, enable the judiciary to provide remedies for administrative inefficiencies, when denial of a right as basic as security of the person is infringed by the procedure and administrative structures created by the law itself, the courts are empowered to act.

Secondly, were it nevertheless possible in this case to dissociate purpose and administration, this Court has already held as a matter of law that purpose is not the only appropriate criterion in evaluating the constitutionality of legislation under the Charter. In *R. v. Big M Drug Mart Ltd.*, at p. 331, the Court stated that:

> . . . both purpose and effect are relevant in determining constitutionality; either an unconstitutional purpose or an unconstitutional effect can invalidate legislation.

Even if the purpose of legislation is unobjectionable, the administrative procedures *created by law* to bring that purpose into operation may produce unconstitutional effects, and the legislation should then be struck down. It is important to note that, in speaking of the effects of legislation, the Court in *R. v. Big M Drug Mart Ltd.* was still referring to effects that can invalidate legislation under s. 52 of the Constitution Act, 1982 and not individual effects that might lead a court to provide a personal remedy under s. 24(1) of the Charter. In the present case, the appellants are complaining of the general effects of s. 251. If s. 251 of the Criminal Code does indeed breach s. 7 of the Charter through its general effects, that can be sufficient to invalidate the legislation under s. 52. As an aside, I should note that the appellants have standing to challenge an unconstitutional law if they are liable to conviction for an offence under that law even though the unconstitutional effects are not directed at the appellants *per se*: *R. v. Big M Drug Mart Ltd.*, at p. 313. The standing of the appellants was not challenged by the Crown.

In summary, s. 251 is a law which forces women to carry a foetus to term contrary to their own priorities and aspirations and which imposes serious delay causing increased physical and psychological trauma to those women who meet its criteria. It must, therefore, be determined whether that infringement is accomplished in accordance with the principles of fundamental justice, thereby saving s. 251 under the second part of s. 7.

C. The Principles of Fundamental Justice

Although the "principles of fundamental justice" referred to in s. 7 have both a substantive and a procedural component (*Re B.C. Motor Vehicle Act*, at p. 499), I have already indicated that it is not necessary in this appeal to evaluate the substantive content of s. 251 of the Criminal Code. My discussion will therefore be limited to various aspects of the administrative structure and procedure set down in s. 251 for access to therapeutic abortions.

In outline, s. 251 operates in the following manner. Subsection (1) creates an indictable offence for any person to use any means with the intent "to procure the miscarriage of a female person". Subsection (2) establishes a parallel indictable offence for any pregnant woman to use or to permit any means to be used with the intent "to procure her own miscarriage". The "means" referred to in subss. (1) and (2) are defined in subs. (3) as the administration of a drug or "other noxious thing", the use of an instrument, and "manipulation of any kind". The crucial provision for the purposes of the present appeal is subs. (4) which states that the offences created in subss. (1) and (2) "do not apply" in certain circumstances. The Ontario Court of Appeal in the proceedings below characterized s. 251(4) as an "exculpatory provision" ((1985), 52 O.R. (2d) 353, at p. 365). In *Morgentaler (1975)*, at p. 673, a majority of this Court held that the effect of s. 251(4) was to afford "a complete answer and defence to those who respect its terms".

The procedure surrounding the defence is rather complex. A pregnant woman who desires to have an abortion must apply to the "therapeutic abortion committee" of an "accredited or approved hospital". Such a committee is empowered to issue a certificate in writing stating that in the opinion of a majority of the committee, the continuation of the pregnancy would be likely to endanger the pregnant woman's life or health. Once a copy of the certificate is given to a qualified medical practitioner who is not a member of the therapeutic abortion committee, he or she is permitted to perform an abortion on the pregnant woman and both the doctor and the woman are freed from any criminal liability.

A number of definitions are provided in subs. (6) which have a bearing on the disposition of this appeal. An "accredited hospital" is described as a hospital accredited by the Canadian Council on Hospital Accreditation "in which diagnostic services and medical, surgical and obstetrical treatment" are provided. An "approved hospital" is a hospital "approved for the purposes of this section by the Minister of Health" of a province. A "therapeutic abortion committee" must be "comprised of not less than three members each of whom is a qualified medical practitioner" who is appointed by the hospital's administrative board. Interestingly, the term "health" is not defined for the purposes of s. 251, so it would appear that the therapeutic abortion committees are free to develop their own theories as to when a potential impairment of a woman's "health" would justify the granting of a therapeutic abortion certificate.

As is so often the case in matters of interpretation, however, the straightforward reading of this statutory scheme is not fully revealing. In order to understand the true nature and scope of s. 251, it is necessary to investigate the practical operation of the provisions. The Court has been provided with a myriad of factual submissions in this area. One of the most useful sources of information is the *Badgley Report*. The Committee on the Operation of the Abortion Law was established by

Orders-in-Council P.C. 1975-2305, -2306, and -2307 of September 29, 1975 and its terms of reference instructed it to "conduct a study to determine whether the procedure provided in the Criminal Code for obtaining therapeutic abortions is operating equitably across Canada". Statistics were provided to the Committee by Statistics Canada and the Committee conducted its own research, meeting with officials of the departments of the provincial attorneys general and of health, and visiting 140 hospitals throughout Canada. The Committee also commissioned national hospital, hospital staff, physician, and patient surveys. The overall conclusion of the Committee was that "the procedures set out for the operation of the Abortion Law are not working equitably across Canada" (p. 17). Of course, that conclusion does not lead to the necessary inference that s. 251 procedures violate the principles of fundamental justice. Unfair functioning of the law could be caused by external forces which do not relate to the law itself.

The *Badgley Report* contains a wealth of detailed information which demonstrates, however, that many of the most serious problems with the functioning of s. 251 are created by procedural and administrative requirements established in the law. For example, the Badgley Committee noted, at p. 84, that

> . . . the Abortion Law implicitly establishes a minimum requirement of three qualified physicians to serve on a therapeutic abortion committee, plus a qualified medical practitioner who is not a member of the therapeutic abortion committee, to perform the procedure.

The Committee went on to make the following observation at p. 102:

> Of the 1,348 civilian hospitals in operation in 1976, at least 331 hospitals had less than four physicians on their medical staff. In terms of the distribution of

physicians, 24.6 percent of hospitals in Canada did not have a medical staff which was large enough to establish a therapeutic abortion committee and to perform the abortion procedure.

In other words, the seemingly neutral requirement of s. 251(4) that at least four physicians be available to authorize and to perform an abortion meant in practice that abortions would be absolutely unavailable in almost one quarter of all hospitals in Canada.

Other administrative and procedural requirements of s. 251(4) reduce the availability of therapeutic abortions even further. For the purposes of s. 251, therapeutic abortions can only be performed in "accredited" or "approved" hospitals. As noted above, an "approved" hospital is one which a provincial minister of health has designated as such for the purpose of performing therapeutic abortions. The minister is under no obligation to grant any such approval. Furthermore, an "accredited" hospital must not only be accredited by the Canadian Council on Hospital Accreditation, it must also provide specified services. Many Canadian hospitals do not provide all of the required services, thereby being automatically disqualified from undertaking therapeutic abortions. The *Badgley Report* stressed the remarkable limitations created by these requirements, especially when linked with the four-physician rule discussed above (p. 105):

> Of the total of 1,348 non-military hospitals in Canada in 1976, 789 hospitals, or 58.5 percent, were ineligible in terms of their major treatment functions, the size of their medical staff, or their type of facility to establish therapeutic abortion committees.

Moreover, even if a hospital is eligible to create a therapeutic abortion committee, there is no requirement in s. 251 that the hospital need do so. The Badgley Committee discovered that in 1976, of the 559 general hospitals which met the procedural requirements of s. 251, only 271 hospitals in Canada, or only 20.1 per cent of the total, had actually established a therapeutic abortion committee (p. 105).

Even though the *Badgley Report* was issued ten years ago, the relevant statistics do not appear to be out of date. Indeed, Statistics Canada reported that in 1982 the number of hospitals with therapeutic abortion committees had actually fallen to 261. (Statistics Canada, *Basic Facts on Therapeutic Abortions, Canada: 1982* (Minister of Supply and Services Canada, 1983)). Even more recent data exists for Ontario. In the *Powell Report*, it was noted that in 1986 only 54 per cent of accredited acute care hospitals in the province had therapeutic abortion committees. In five counties there were no committees at all (p. 24). Of the ninety-five hospitals with committees, twelve did not do any abortions in 1986 (p. 24).

The *Powell Report* reveals another serious difficulty with s. 251 procedures. The requirement that therapeutic abortions be performed only in "accredited" or "approved" hospitals effectively means that the practical availability of the exculpatory provisions of subs. (4) may be heavily restricted, even denied, through provincial regulation. In Ontario, for example, the provincial government promulgated O. Reg. 248/70 under The Public Hospitals Act, R.S.O. 1960, c. 322, now R.R.O. 1980, Reg. 865. This regulation provides that therapeutic abortion committees can only be established where there are ten or more members on the active medical staff (*Powell Report*, at p. 13). A Minister of Health is not prevented from imposing harsher restrictions. During argument, it was noted that it would even be possible for a provincial government, exercising its legislative authority over public hospitals, to distribute funding for treatment facilities in such a way that no hospital would meet the procedural requirements of s.

251(4). Because of the administrative structure established in s. 251(4) and the related definitions, the "defence" created in the section could be completely wiped out.

A further flaw with the administrative system established in s. 251(4) is the failure to provide an adequate standard for therapeutic abortion committees which must determine when a therapeutic abortion should, as a matter of law, be granted. Subsection (4) states simply that a therapeutic abortion committee may grant a certificate when it determines that a continuation of a pregnancy would be likely to endanger the "life or health" of the pregnant woman. It was noted above that "health" is not defined for the purposes of the section. The Crown admitted in its supplementary factum that the medical witnesses at trial testified uniformly that the "health" standard was ambiguous, but the Crown derives comfort from the fact that "the medical witnesses were unanimous in their approval of the broad World Health Organization definition of health". The World Health Organization defines "health" not merely as the absence of disease or infirmity, but as a state of physical, mental and social well-being.

I do not understand how the mere existence of a workable definition of "health" can make the use of the word in s. 251(4) any less ambiguous when that definition is nowhere referred to in the section. There is no evidence that therapeutic abortion committees are commonly applying the World Health Organization definition. Indeed, the Badgley Report indicates that the situation is quite the contrary (p. 20):

> There has been no sustained or firm effort in Canada to develop an explicit and operational definition of health, or to apply such a concept directly to the operation of induced abortion. In the absence of such a definition, each physician and each hospital reaches an individual decision on this matter. How the concept of

health is variably defined leads to considerable inequity in the distribution and the accessibility of the abortion procedure.

Various expert doctors testified at trial that therapeutic abortion committees apply widely differing definitions of health. For some committees, psychological health is a justification for therapeutic abortion; for others it is not. Some committees routinely refuse abortions to married women unless they are in physical danger, while for other committees it is possible for a married woman to show that she would suffer psychological harm if she continued with a pregnancy, thereby justifying an abortion. It is not typically possible for women to know in advance what standard of health will be applied by any given committee. Parker A.C.J.H.C., at p. 377, found clear evidence that s. 251(4) provided no adequate guidelines for therapeutic abortion committees charged with determining when an abortion should legally be available:

> The [*Badgley*] report, and other evidence adduced in support of this motion, indicates that each therapeutic abortion committee is free to establish its own guidelines and many committees apply arbitrary requirements. Some committees refuse to approve applications for second abortions unless the patient consents to sterilization, others require psychiatric assessment, and others do not grant approval to married women.

It is no answer to say that "health" is a medical term and that doctors who sit on therapeutic abortion committees must simply exercise their professional judgment. A therapeutic abortion committee is a strange hybrid, part medical committee and part legal committee. Again, in the words of Parker A.C.J.H.C. at p. 381:

Given the consequences of the issuing or refusing to issue a certificate, I have some difficulty in reducing the committee's powers to merely that of stating its opinion as to the likelihood of the continuation of the pregnancy endangering the applicant's life or health. The decision of the committee has a very real effect on access to abortion for the pregnant female applicant, and the potential criminal liability of both the applicant and the physician who performs the operation.

When the decision of the therapeutic abortion committee is so directly laden with legal consequences, the absence of any clear legal standard to be applied by the committee in reaching its decision is a serious procedural flaw.

The combined effect of all of these problems with the procedure stipulated in s. 251 for access to therapeutic abortions is a failure to comply with the principles of fundamental justice. In Re B.C. Motor Vehicle Act, Lamer J. held, at p. 503, that "the principles of fundamental justice are to be found in the basic tenets of our legal system". One of the basic tenets of our system of criminal justice is that when Parliament creates a defence to a criminal charge, the defence should not be illusory or so difficult to attain as to be practically illusory. The criminal law is a very special form of governmental regulation, for it seeks to express our society's collective disapprobation of certain acts and omissions. When a defence is provided, especially a specifically-tailored defence to a particular charge, it is because the legislator has determined that the disapprobation of society is not warranted when the conditions of the defence are met.

Consider then the case of a pregnant married woman who wishes to apply for a therapeutic abortion certificate because she fears that her psychological health would be impaired seriously if she carried the foetus to term. The uncontroverted evidence reveals that there are many areas in Canada where such a woman would simply not have access to a therapeutic abortion. She may live in an area where no hospital has four doctors; no therapeutic abortion committee can be created. Equally, she may live in a place where the treatment functions of the nearby hospitals do not satisfy the definition of "accredited hospital" in s. 251(6). Or she may live in a province where the provincial government has imposed such stringent requirements on hospitals seeking to create therapeutic abortion committees that no hospital can qualify. Alternatively, our hypothetical woman may confront a therapeutic abortion committee in her local hospital which defines "health" in purely physical terms or which refuses to countenance abortions for married women. In each of these cases, it is the administrative structures and procedures established by s. 251 itself that would in practice prevent the woman from gaining the benefit of the defence held out to her in s. 251(4).

The facts indicate that many women do indeed confront these problems. Doctors from the Chedoke-McMaster Hospital in Hamilton testified that they received telephone calls from women throughout Ontario who had applied for therapeutic abortions at local hospitals and been refused. At one point, eighty per cent of abortion patients at Chedoke-McMaster were from outside Hamilton, and the hospital was forced to restrict access for women from outside its catchment area. The *Powell Report* revealed that in over fifty per cent of Ontario counties in 1986, the majority of women obtaining abortions had the procedure away from their place of residence (p. 7). Even more telling is the fact that "a minimum of 5000 Ontario women obtain abortions each year in freestanding clinics in Canada and the United States" (p. 7).

The Crown argues in its supplementary factum that women who face difficulties in obtaining abortions at home can simply travel elsewhere in Canada to procure a therapeutic abortion. That submission would not be especially troubling if the difficulties facing women were not in large measure created by the procedural requirements of s. 251 itself. If women were seeking anonymity outside their home town or were simply confronting the reality that it is often difficult to obtain medical services in rural areas, it might be appropriate to say "let them travel". But the evidence establishes convincingly that it is the law itself which in many ways *prevents* access to local therapeutic abortion facilities. The enormous emotional and financial burden placed upon women who must travel long distances from home to obtain an abortion is a burden created in many instances by Parliament. Moreover, it is not accurate to say to women who would seem to qualify under s. 251(4) that they can get a therapeutic abortion as long as they are willing to travel. Ms. Carolyn Egan, administrative co-ordinator of the Birth Control and Venereal Disease Centre of Toronto, testified that many hospitals in Toronto had been forced to establish arbitrary abortion quotas, and that some Toronto hospitals restricted access to women inside the geographical area the hospitals were designated to serve. A woman from outside Toronto could run into serious difficulties attempting to procure a therapeutic abortion in that city. As noted above, the situation of Hamilton is now comparable to that in Toronto, because of the geographic restrictions imposed at the Chedoke-McMaster Hospital. Meanwhile, of course, days and weeks may pass and a woman may ultimately be forced to undergo a more dangerous abortion procedure. Or she may become desperate and choose to travel even further afield, to Quebec or to the United States, to obtain an abortion in a free-standing clinic.

A majority of this Court held in *R. v. Jones*, at p. 304, *per* La Forest J., that

The provinces must be given room to make choices regarding the type of administrative structure that will suit their needs unless the use of such structure is in itself so manifestly unfair, having regard to the decisions it is called upon to make, as to violate the principles of *fundamental* justice. [Emphasis in original.]

Similarly, Parliament must be given room to design an appropriate administrative and procedural structure for bringing into operation a particular defence to criminal liability. But if that structure is "so manifestly unfair, having regard to the decisions it is called upon to make, as to violate the principles of *fundamental* justice", that structure must be struck down. In the present case, the structure — the system regulating access to therapeutic abortions — is manifestly unfair. It contains so many potential barriers to its own operation that the defence it creates will in many circumstances be practically unavailable to women who would *prima facie* qualify for the defence, or at least would force such women to travel great distances at substantial expense and inconvenience in order to benefit from a defence that is held out to be generally available.

I conclude that the procedures created in s. 251 of the Criminal Code for obtaining a therapeutic abortion do not comport with the principles of fundamental justice. It is not necessary to determine whether s. 7 also contains a substantive content leading to the conclusion that, in some circumstances at least, the deprivation of a pregnant woman's right to security of the person can never comport with fundamental justice. Simply put, assuming Parliament can act, it must do so properly. For the reasons given earlier, the deprivation of security of the person caused by s. 251 as a whole is not in accordance with the second clause of s. 7. It remains to be seen whether s. 251 can be justified for the purposes of s. 1 of the Charter.

V. Section 1 Analysis

Section 1 of the Charter can potentially be used to "salvage" a legislative provision which breaches s. 7: *Re B.C. Motor Vehicle Act*, *per* Lamer J., at p. 520. The principles governing the necessary analysis under s. 1 were set down in *R. v. Big M Drug Mart Ltd.*, and, more precisely, in *R. v. Oakes*, [1986] 1 S.C.R. 103. A statutory provision which infringes any section of the Charter can only be saved under s. 1 if the party seeking to uphold the provision can demonstrate first, that the objective of the provision is "of sufficient importance to warrant overriding a constitutionally protected right or freedom" (*R. v. Big M Drug Mart Ltd.*, at p. 352) and second, that the means chosen in overriding the right or freedom are reasonable and demonstrably justified in a free and democratic society. This second aspect ensures that the legislative means are proportional to the legislative ends (*Oakes*, at pp. 139-40). In *Oakes*, at p. 139, the Court referred to three considerations which are typically useful in assessing the proportionality of means to ends. First, the means chosen to achieve an important objective should be rational, fair and not arbitrary. Second, the legislative means should impair as little as possible the right or freedom under consideration. Third, the effects of the limitation upon the relevant right or freedom should not be out of proportion to the objective sought to be achieved.

The appellants contended that the sole purpose of s. 251 of the Criminal Code is to protect the life and health of pregnant women. The respondent Crown submitted that s. 251 seeks to protect not only the life and health of pregnant women, but also the interests of the foetus. On the other hand, the Crown conceded that the Court is not called upon in this appeal to evaluate any claim to "foetal rights" or to assess the meaning of "the right to life". I expressly refrain from so doing. In my view, it is unnecessary for the purpose of deciding this appeal to evaluate or assess "foetal rights" as an independent constitutional value. Nor are we required to measure the full extent of the state's interest in establishing criteria unrelated to the pregnant woman's own priorities and aspirations. What we must do is evaluate the particular balance struck by Parliament in s. 251, as it relates to the priorities and aspirations of pregnant women and the government's interests in the protection of the foetus.

Section 251 provides that foetal interests are not to be protected where the "life or health" of the woman is threatened. Thus, Parliament itself has expressly stated in s. 251 that the "life or health" of pregnant women is paramount. The procedures of s. 251(4) are clearly related to the pregnant woman's "life or health" for that is the very phrase used by the subsection. As McIntyre J. states in his reasons, the aim of s. 251(4) is "to restrict abortion to cases where the continuation of the pregnancy would, or would likely, be injurious to the life or health of the woman concerned, not to provide unrestricted access to abortion." I have no difficulty in concluding that the objective of s. 251 as a whole, namely, to balance the competing interests identified by Parliament, is sufficiently important to meet the requirements of the first step in the *Oakes* inquiry under s. 1. I think the protection of the interests of pregnant women is a valid governmental objective, where life and health can be jeopardized by criminal sanctions. Like Beetz and Wilson JJ., I agree that protection of foetal interests by Parliament is also a valid governmental objective. It follows that balancing these interests, with the lives and health of women a major factor, is clearly an important governmental objective. As the Court of Appeal stated, "the contemporary view [is] that abortion is not always socially undesirable behavior."

I am equally convinced, however, that the means chosen to advance the legislative objectives of s. 251 do not satisfy any of the three elements of the proportionality component of *R. v. Oakes*. The evidence has led me to conclude that the infringement of the security of the person of pregnant women caused by s. 251 is not accomplished in accordance with the principles of fundamental justice. It has been demonstrated that the procedures and administrative structures created by s. 251 are often arbitrary and unfair. The procedures established to implement the policy of s. 251 impair s. 7 rights far more than is necessary because they hold out an illusory defence to many women who would *prima facie* qualify under the exculpatory provisions of s. 251(4). In other words, many women whom Parliament professes not to wish to subject to criminal liability will nevertheless be forced by the practical unavailability of the supposed defence to risk liability or to suffer other harm such as a traumatic late abortion caused by the delay inherent in the s. 251 system. Finally, the effects of the limitation upon the s. 7 rights of many pregnant women are out of proportion to the objective sought to be achieved. Indeed, to the extent that s. 251(4) is designed to protect the life and health of women, the procedures it establishes may actually defeat the objective. The administrative structures of s. 251(4) are so cumbersome that women whose health is endangered by pregnancy may not be able to gain a therapeutic abortion, at least without great trauma, expense and inconvenience.

I conclude, therefore, that the cumbersome structure of subs. (4) not only unduly subordinates the s. 7 rights of pregnant women but may also defeat the value Parliament itself has established as paramount, namely, the life and health of the mother. As I have noted, counsel for the Crown did contend that one purpose of the procedures required by subs. (4) is to protect the interests of the foetus. State protection of foetal interests may well be deserving of constitutional recognition under s. 1. Still, there can be no escape from the fact that Parliament has failed to establish either a standard or a procedure whereby any such interests might prevail over those of the woman in a fair and non-arbitrary fashion.

Section 251 of the Criminal Code cannot be saved, therefore, under s. 1 of the Charter.

VI. Defence Counsel's Address to the Jury

In his concluding remarks to the jury at the trial of the appellants, defence counsel asserted:

> The judge will tell you what the law is. He will tell you about the ingredients of the offence, what the Crown has to prove, what the defences may be or may not be, and you must take the law from him. But I submit to you that it is up to you and you alone to apply the law to this evidence and you have a right to say it shouldn't be applied.

The burden of his argument was that the jury should not apply s. 251 if they thought that it was a bad law, and that, in refusing to apply the law, they could send a signal to Parliament that the law should be changed. Although my disposition of the appeal makes it unnecessary, strictly speaking, to review Mr. Manning's argument before the jury, I find the argument so troubling that I feel compelled to comment.

It has long been settled in Anglo-Canadian criminal law that in a trial before judge and jury, the judge's role is to state the law and the jury's role is to apply that law to the facts of the case. In *Joshua v. The Queen*, [1955] A.C. 121 (P.C.), at p. 130, Lord Oaksey enunciated the principle succinctly:

> It is a general principle of British law that on a trial by jury it is for the judge to direct the jury on the law and in

so far as he thinks necessary on the facts, but the jury, whilst they must take the law from the judge, are the sole judges on the facts.

The jury is one of the great protectors of the citizen because it is composed of twelve persons who collectively express the common sense of the community. But the jury members are not expert in the law, and for that reason they must be guided by the judge on questions of law.

The contrary principle contended for by Mr. Manning, that a jury may be encouraged to ignore a law it does not like, could lead to gross inequities. One accused could be convicted by a jury who supported the existing law, while another person indicted for the same offence could be acquitted by a jury who, with reformist zeal, wished to express disapproval of the same law. Moreover, a jury could decide that although the law pointed to a conviction, the jury would simply refuse to apply the law to an accused for whom it had sympathy. Alternatively, a jury who feels antipathy towards an accused might convict despite a law which points to acquittal. To give a harsh but I think telling example, a jury fueled by the passions of racism could be told that they need not apply the law against murder to a white man who had killed a black man. Such a possibility need only be stated to reveal the potentially frightening implications of Mr. Manning's assertions. The dangerous argument that a jury may be encouraged to disregard the law was castigated as long ago as 1784 by Lord Mansfield in a criminal libel case, *R. v. Shipley* (1784), 4 Dougl. 73, 99 E.R. 774, at p. 824:

> So the jury who usurp the judicature of law, though they happen to be right, are themselves wrong, because they are right by chance only, and have not taken the constitutional way of deciding the question. It is the duty of the Judge, in all cases of general justice, to tell the jury how to do right, though they have it in their

power to do wrong, which is a matter entirely between God and their own consciences.

To be free is to live under a government by law. . . . Miserable is the condition of individuals, dangerous is the condition of the State, if there is no certain law, or, which is the same thing, no certain administration of law, to protect individuals, or to guard the State. . . .

In opposition to this, what is contended for? — That the law shall be, in every particular cause, what any twelve men, who shall happen to be the jury, shall be inclined to think; liable to no review, and subject to no control, under all the prejudices of the popular cry of the day, and under all the bias of interest in this town, where thousands, more or less, are concerned in the publication of newspapers, paragraphs, and pamphlets. Under such an administration of law, no man could tell, no counsel could advise, whether a paper was or was not punishable.

I can only add my support to that eloquent statement of principle.

It is no doubt true that juries have a *de facto* power to disregard the law as stated to the jury by the judge. We cannot enter the jury room. The jury is never called upon to explain the reasons which lie behind a verdict. It may even be true that in some limited circumstances the private decision of a jury to refuse to apply the law will constitute, in the words of a Law Reform Commission of Canada working paper, "the citizen's ultimate protection against oppressive laws and the oppressive enforcement of the law" (Law Reform Commission of Canada, Working Paper 27, *The Jury in Criminal Trials* (1980)). But recognizing this reality is a far cry from suggesting that counsel may encourage a jury to ignore a law they do not support or to tell a jury that it has a right to do so. The difference between accepting the reality of *de facto* discretion in applying the law and elevating such discretion to the level of a right was stated clearly by the United States Court of Appeals, District of Columbia

Circuit, in *U.S. v. Dougherty*, 473 F.2d 1113 (1972), *per* Leventhal J., at p. 1134:

> The jury system has worked out reasonably well overall, providing "play in the joints" that imparts flexibility and avoid[s] undue rigidity. An equilibrium has evolved — an often marvelous balance — with the jury acting as a "safety valve" for exceptional cases, without being a wildcat or runaway institution. There is reason to believe that the simultaneous achievement of modest jury equity and avoidance of intolerable caprice depends on formal instructions that do not expressly delineate a jury charter to carve out its own rules of law.

To accept Mr. Mannning's argument that defence counsel should be able to encourage juries to ignore the law would be to disturb the "marvelous balance" of our system of criminal trials before a judge and jury. Such a disturbance would be irresponsible. I agree with the trial judge and with the Court of Appeal that Mr. Manning was quite simply wrong to say to the jury that if they did not like the law they need not enforce it. He should not have done so.

VII. Conclusion

Section 251 of the Criminal Code infringes the right to security of the person of many pregnant women. The procedures and administrative structures established in the section to provide for therapeutic abortions do not comply with the principles of fundamental justice. Section 7 of the Charter is infringed and that infringement cannot be saved under s. 1.

In oral argument, counsel for the Crown submitted that if the Court were to hold that procedural aspects of s. 251 infringed the Charter, only the procedures set out in the section should be struck down, that is subss. (4) and (5). After being pressed with questions from the bench, Ms. Wein conceded that the whole of s. 251 should fall if it infringed s. 7. Mr. Blacklock for the Attorney General of Canada took the same position. This was a wise approach, for in *Morgentaler (1975)*, at p. 676, the Court held that "s. 251 contains a comprehensive code on the subject of abortions, unitary and complete within itself". Having found that this "comprehensive code" infringes the Charter, it is not the role of the Court to pick and choose among the various aspects of s. 251 so as effectively to re-draft the section. The appeal should therefore be allowed and s. 251 as a whole struck down under s. 52(1) of the Constitution Act, 1982.

The first constitutional question is therefore answered in the affirmative as regards s. 7 of the Charter only. The second question, as regards s. 7 of the Charter only, is answered in the negative. Questions 3, 4 and 5 are answered in the negative. I answer question 6 in the manner proposed by Beetz J. It is not necessary to answer question 7.

Reasons for Judgment:
Justice Jean Beetz

Concurred in by
*   Justice Willard Estey*

I have had the advantage of reading the reasons for judgment written by the Chief Justice, as well as the reasons written by Mr. Justice McIntyre and Madame Justice Wilson.

I agree with the Chief Justice and Wilson J. that this case finds its resolution in the answers to the first constitutional questions stated by the Chief Justice in so far as those questions relate to s. 7 and s. 1 of the Charter. Although the greatest part of my reasons is devoted to responding to the first two constitutional questions, I consider it necessary to answer the sixth constitutional question concerning the validity of para. 605(1)(*a*) of the Criminal Code under the Charter in order to establish the Crown's right to appeal the verdict of acquittal in this case. Finally, I have decided that it is appropriate to address the appellants' arguments pertaining to s. 91(27) and s. 96 of the Constitution Act, 1867, as well as the argument that s. 251 of the Criminal Code is in effect an unconstitutional delegation of legislative power.

Like the Chief Justice and Wilson J., I would allow the appeal and answer the first constitutional question in the affirmative and the second constitutional question in the negative. This however is a result which I reach for reasons which differ from those of the Chief Justice and those of Wilson J.

I find it convenient to outline at the outset the steps which lead me to this result:

I — Before the advent of the Charter, Parliament recognized, in adopting subs. 251(4) of the Criminal Code, that the interest in the life or health of the pregnant woman takes precedence over the interest in prohibiting abortions, including the interest of the state in the protection of the foetus, when "the continuation of the pregnancy of such female person would or would be likely to endanger her life or health". In my view, this standard in subs. 251(4) became entrenched at least as a minimum when the "right to life, liberty and security of the person" was enshrined in the Canadian Charter of Rights and Freedoms at s. 7.

II — "Security of the person" within the meaning of s. 7 of the Charter must include a right of access to medical treatment for a condition representing a danger to life or health without fear of criminal sanction. If an act of Parliament forces a pregnant woman whose life or health is in danger to choose between, on the one hand, the commission of a crime to obtain effective and timely medical treatment and, on the other hand, inadequate treatment or no treatment at all, her right to security of the person has been violated.

III — According to the evidence, the procedural requirements of s. 251 of the Criminal Code significantly delay pregnant women's access to medical treatment resulting in an additional danger to their health, thereby depriving them of their right to security of the person.

IV — The deprivation referred to in the preceding

proposition does not accord with the principles of fundamental justice. While Parliament is justified in requiring a reliable, independent and medically sound opinion as to the "life or health" of the pregnant woman in order to protect the state interest in the foetus, and while any such statutory mechanism will inevitably result in some delay, certain of the procedural requirements of s. 251 of the Criminal Code are nevertheless manifestly unfair. These requirements are manifestly unfair in that they are unnecessary in respect of Parliament's objectives in establishing the administrative structure *and* that they result in additional risks to the health of pregnant women.

V — The primary objective of s. 251 of the Criminal Code is the protection of the foetus. The protection of the life and health of the pregnant woman is an ancillary objective. The primary objective does relate to concerns which are pressing and substantial in a free and democratic society and which, pursuant to s. 1 of the Charter, justify reasonable limits to be put on a woman's right. However, rules unnecessary in respect of the primary and ancillary objectives which they are designed to serve, such as some of the rules contained in s. 251, cannot be said to be rationally connected to these objectives under s. 1 of the Charter. Consequently, s. 251 does not constitute a reasonable limit to the security of the person.

It is not necessary to decide whether there is a proportionality between the effects of s. 251 and the objective of protecting the foetus, nor is it necessary to answer the question concerning the circumstances in which there is a proportionality between the effects of s. 251 which limit the right of pregnant women to security of the person and the objective of the protection of the foetus. But I feel bound to observe that the objective of protecting the foetus would not justify the severity of the breach of pregnant women's right to security of the person which would result if the exculpatory provision of s. 251 was *completely* removed from the Criminal Code. However, a rule that would require a higher degree of danger to health in the latter months of pregnancy, as opposed to the early months, for an abortion to be lawful, could possibly achieve a proportionality which would be acceptable under s. 1 of the Charter.

I. Section 251 of the Criminal Code

[Justice Beetz here reproduces Section 251 of the Criminal Code, which the reader can find in Chief Justice Dickson's Reasons for Judgment, pages 28-31.]

Subsection (1) defines the indictable offence committed when a person uses any means for the purpose of carrying out his or her intention of procuring the miscarriage of a female person. Subsection (2) states that a pregnant woman who uses any means or permits any means to be used for the purpose of procuring her own miscarriage is guilty of an indictable offence with a lesser maximum penalty. Subsection (3) defines the expression "means" for s. 251.

Subsection (4), when read in conjunction with subsections (5), (6) and (7), outlines the circumstances in which an abortion can be lawfully performed. For the purposes of this appeal in which the existence of a constitutional right of access to abortion and the extent of that right is in issue, it is of special importance to understand the circumstances in which Parliament decriminalized abortion and thereby rendered it available without criminal sanction under ordinary law. Indeed, before the advent of the Charter, Parliament recognized that the interest in the life or health of the pregnant woman takes precedence over the interest in prohibiting abortions, including the interest of the state in the protection of the foetus, when the continuation of the pregnancy would or would be likely to endanger the pregnant woman's life or health. Access to lawful abortion under the Criminal Code, albeit in limited circumstances, exists independently of any right which may or may not be founded upon the Charter.

As its opening words make plain, subsection (4) is an exculpatory provision: subsections (1) and (2), which indicate when conduct related to procuring a miscarriage is an indictable offence, "do not apply" when the terms of subsection (4) are respected. Until s. 18 of the Criminal Law Amendment Act, 1968-69, S.C. 1968-69, c. 37 added subsections (4), (5), (6) and (7), there was no statutory exception to the crime of abortion. In the case at bar, the Ontario Court of Appeal explained the historical significance of the adoption in 1969 of these exculpatory provisions in the following terms:

> By defining criminal conduct more narrowly, these amendments reflected the contemporary view that abortion is not always socially undesirable behaviour.

(1985), 22 C.C.C. (3d) 353 at 365.

Access to abortion without risk of criminal penalty under the Criminal Code is expressed by Parliament in subs. 251(4), (5), (6) and (7) as relieving provisions in respect of the indictable offences defined at subsections 251(1) and (2). According to Laskin C.J. (dissenting) in *Morgentaler v. The Queen*, [1976] 1 S.C.R. 616 [hereinafter *Morgentaler (1975)*], these relieving provisions "simply permit a person to make conduct lawful which would otherwise be unlawful" (at 631). In the same case, Pigeon J. said that in 1969 "an explicit and specific definition was made of the circumstances under which an abortion could lawfully be performed" (at 660).

What is important, for our purposes, in considering subsection (4) is not, of course, the name we give to the exculpatory rule but the rule itself: Parliament has recognized that circumstances exist in which an abortion

69

can be procured lawfully. The Court of Appeal observed at *supra*, 378:

> A woman's only right to an abortion at the time the
> Charter came into force would accordingly appear to
> be that given to ss. (4) of s. 251.

Given that it appears in a criminal law statute, subs. 251(4) cannot be said to create a "right", much less a constitutional right, but it does represent an exception decreed by Parliament pursuant to what the Court of Appeal aptly called "the contemporary view that abortion is not always socially undesirable behaviour". Examining the content of the rule by which Parliament decriminalizes abortion is the most appropriate first step in considering the validity of s. 251 as against the constitutional right alleged by the appellants in argument.

By enacting subs. 251(4), (5), (6) and (7) in 1969, Parliament endeavoured to decriminalize abortion in one circumstance, described in substantive terms in para. 251(4)(*c*): when the continuation of the pregnancy of the woman would or would be likely to endanger her life or health. This is the crux of the exception. This is the circumstance in which Parliament decided to allow women to procure a miscarriage without criminal sanction either for themselves or for their doctors. Chief Justice Laskin referred to this "would or would be likely to endanger her life or health" element in para. 251(4)(*c*) as the "standard in s. 251(4)" in *Morgentaler (1975)*, *supra*, at 629.

The remaining provisions of subs. 251(4), (5), (6) and (7) are designed to ascertain whether the standard has been met in a given case. To employ the expression of the Attorney General of Canada who intervened in this case in defence of s. 251, these provisions were designed, in part, "to allow relief from criminal sanction where there is reliable, independent and medically sound judgment that the life or health of the mother would be or would likely be endangered . . . " Paragraph 251(4)(*a*) requires, for example, that a therapeutic abortion committee give its opinion in writing that the standard has been met. The committee is comprised of not less than three qualified medical practitioners appointed by the board of the hospital where the treatment would take place. The qualified medical practitioner who would perform the abortion may not be a member of a therapeutic abortion committee for any hospital. The opinion must be that of the majority of the members of the committee and must be made by certificate in writing and given to the practitioner who, according to para. 251(4)(*a*), must be in "good faith" and, consequently, have no reason to believe that the standard in para. 251(4)(*c*) has not been met. The Minister of Health of the province in which the certificate was issued may by order require the therapeutic abortion committee to furnish him with a copy of the certificate. Other aspects of subs. 251(4) are designed to ensure the safety of the abortion itself *after* the standard has been met and *after* the certificate to this effect has been issued enabling the woman to have a lawful abortion. These include the requirements that the practitioner be properly qualified and that the abortion be carried out in an accredited or approved hospital.

Overall, the procedure set forth at subs. 251(4) is in place to ensure that the standard of the exception — that the continuation of the pregnancy would or would be likely to endanger the pregnant woman's health — is met before Parliament will allow an abortion to be performed without punishment. Parliament will protect the life and health of the pregnant woman by allowing her access to an abortion when it has been established, through the means selected by Parliament, that her life or health would or would likely be in danger if her pregnancy continued. The other provisions in subs. 251(4), though necessary for an abortion to be lawful, were enacted to ensure that the standard was met and that, once met, the lawful abortion would be performed safely. These other rules are a means to an end and not an end unto themselves. As a whole, subs. 251(4), (5), (6) and (7) seek to make therapeutic abortions lawful and available but also to ensure that the excuse of therapy will not be abused and that lawful abortions be safe.

That abortions are recognized as lawful by Parliament based on a specific standard under its ordinary laws is important, I think, to a proper understanding of the existence of a right of access to abortion founded on rights guaranteed by s. 7 of the Charter. The constitutional right does not have its source in the Criminal Code, but, in my view, the content of the standard in subs. 251(4) that Parliament recognized in the Criminal Law Amendment Act, 1969 was for all intents and purposes entrenched at least as a minimum in 1982 when a distinct right in s. 7 became part of Canadian constitutional law.

II. The Right to Security of the Person in s. 7 of the Charter

Section 7 of the Charter provides:

> 7. Everyone has the right to life, liberty and security of the person and the right not to be deprived thereof except in accordance with the principles of fundamental justice.

I share the view first expressed by Wilson J. in *Singh v. Minister of Employment and Immigration*, [1985] 1 S.C.R. 177 at 205 and confirmed by Lamer J. in *Re B.C. Motor Vehicle Act*, [1985] 2 S.C.R. 486 at 500 that "it is incumbent upon this Court to give meaning to each of the elements, life, liberty and security of the person, which make up the 'right' contained in s. 7." The full ambit of this constitutionally protected right will only be revealed over time. Consequently, the minimum content which I attribute to s. 7 does not preclude, or for that matter assure, the finding of a wider constitutional right when the courts will be faced with this or other issues in other contexts. As we shall see, the content of the "security of the person" element of the s. 7 right is sufficient in itself to invalidate s. 251 of the Criminal Code and consequently dispose of the appeal.

In discussing the content of the right protected by s. 7 of the Charter in the case at bar, the Ontario Court of Appeal wrote at p. 377 that "it would place too narrow an interpretation on s. 7 to limit it to protection against arbitrary arrest and detention" (at 377). It will be seen from what follows that I agree with this view. Indeed the natural meaning of "life, liberty and security of the person" belies this limited view of the scope of s. 7. As Estey J. observed in *Law Society of Upper Canada v. Skapinker*, [1984] 1 S.C.R. 357 at 377, examining the "Legal Rights" heading which introduces sections 7 to 14 of the Charter is at best one step in the constitutional interpretation process and is not necessarily of controlling importance. I am mindful, however, that it is in the criminal law context that "security of the person" and the alleged violation of s. 7 arise in this case. Enjoying "security of the person" free from criminal sanction is central to understanding the violation of the Charter right which I describe herein. It is not necessary to decide whether s. 7 would apply in other circumstances.

A pregnant woman's person cannot be said to be secure if, when her life or health is in danger, she is faced with a rule of criminal law which precludes her from obtaining effective and timely medical treatment.

Generally speaking, the constitutional right to security of the person must include some protection from state interference when a person's life or health is in danger. The Charter does not, needless to say, protect men and women from even the most serious misfortunes of nature. Section 7 cannot be invoked simply because a person's life or health is in danger. The state can obviously not be said to have violated, for example, a pregnant woman's security of the person simply on the basis that her pregnancy in and of itself represents a danger to her life or health. There must be state intervention for "security of the person" in s. 7 to be violated.

If a rule of criminal law precludes a person from obtaining appropriate medical treatment when his or her life or health is in danger, then the state has intervened and this intervention constitutes a violation of that man's or that woman's security of the person. "Security of the person" must include a right of access to medical treatment for a condition representing a danger to life or health without fear of criminal sanction. If an act of Parliament forces a person whose life or health is in danger to choose between, on the one hand, the commission of a crime to obtain effective and timely medical treatment and, on the other hand, inadequate treatment or no treatment at all, the right to security of the person has been violated.

This interpretation of s. 7 of the Charter is sufficient to measure the content of s. 251 of the Criminal Code against that of the Charter in order to dispose of this appeal. While I agree with McIntyre J. that a breach of a right to security must be "based upon an infringement of some interest which would be of such nature and such importance as to warrant constitutional protection", I am of the view that the protection of life or health is an interest of sufficient importance in this regard. Under the Criminal Code, the only way in which a pregnant woman can legally secure an abortion when the continuation of the pregnancy would or would be likely to endanger her life or health is to comply with the procedure set forth at subs. 251(4). Where the continued pregnancy does constitute a danger to life or health, the pregnant woman faces a choice: (1) she can endeavour to follow the subs. 251(4) procedure, which, as we shall see, creates an additional medical risk given its inherent delays and the possibility that the danger will not be recognized by the state-imposed therapeutic abortion committee; or (2) she can secure medical treatment without respecting subs. 251(4) and subject herself to criminal sanction under subs. 251(2).

III. Delays Caused by S.251 Procedure in Violation of Security of the Person

This chapter requires a review of the evidence, part of which is to be found in two reports, the *Report of the Committee on the Operation of the Abortion Law* (the *Badgley Report*), and the *Report on Therapeutic Abortion Services in Ontario* (the *Powell Report*).

The *Badgley Report*, Ottawa, Supply and Services Canada, 1977, was written by a committee appointed by the Privy Council with a mandate to conduct a study to determine whether the procedure provided in the Criminal Code for obtaining therapeutic abortions is operating equitably across Canada and to make findings on the operations of this law rather than recommendations on the underlying policy: *Badgley Report* at p. 27.

The *Powell Report*, Toronto, Ministry of Health (Ontario), January 27, 1987, unpublished, is a study commissioned by the Ministry of Health with terms of reference limited to a review of access to therapeutic abortion services in Ontario. Like those for the *Badgley Report*, these terms did not include the mandate for an evaluation of the underlying policy of the Criminal Code: *Powell Report*, Appendix 1.

I propose to consider first the delays caused by s. 251 procedure and then the consequences of the delays.

1. Delays caused by s. 251 procedure

The evidence reveals that the actual workings of subs. 251(4) are the source of certain delays which create an additional medical risk for many pregnant women whose medical condition already meets the standard of para. 251(4)(c). Stated simply, when pregnant women suffer from a condition which represents a danger to their life or health, their efforts to conform to the procedure set forth for obtaining lawful abortions in the Criminal Code often create an additional risk to their health. They may have to choose between bearing the burden of these risks by accepting delayed medical treatment, and committing a crime by seeking timely medical treatment outside subs. 251(4). Given that the procedure in subs. 251(4) is the source of this additional risk, it constitutes a violation of the pregnant woman's security of the person. I shall first endeavour to show that these delays have their origin in s. 251. I will then cite evidence that these procedural delays create an additional risk to the health of pregnant women.

While only administrative inefficiencies that are caused by the rules in s. 251 are relevant to the evaluation of the constitutionality of the legislation under s. 7 of the Charter, the evidence which relates to the availability of therapeutic abortions under the Criminal Code reveals three sorts of delay, *all of which can be traced to the requirements of s. 251 itself*: (1) the absence of hospitals with therapeutic abortion committees in many parts of Canada; (2) the quotas which some hospitals with committees impose on the number of therapeutic abortions which they perform and (3) the committee requirement itself each create delays for pregnant women who seek timely and effective medical treatment.

(1) Lack of hospitals with therapeutic abortion committees

Hospitals with therapeutic abortion committees are

completely lacking in many parts of Canada, forcing women to go elsewhere and suffer delays in order to gain access to hospitals in which they may obtain therapeutic abortions free from criminal sanction. The requirements which hospitals must meet under s. 251 are responsible for this absence of eligible hospitals. Often, the absence of hospitals can be traced to the prerequisites which hospitals must meet under subs. 251(6). In other cases, the absence is caused by the refusal of certain hospital boards to appoint committees in hospitals which would otherwise qualify under the law, as is their prerogative under subs. 251(6). I shall consider each of these in turn.

The effect of certain definitions in subs. 251(6), when read in conjunction with subs. 251(4), is to cause an absence of hospitals in which therapeutic abortions can legally be performed. A "therapeutic abortion committee" for any hospital means, according to subs. 251(6), a committee comprised of not less than three physicians from which the physician who performs the abortion is excluded under subs. 251(4). As the Chief Justice observed, the combined effect of these two provisions is to require at least four physicians at the hospital so that the therapeutic abortion can be lawfully authorized and performed. The four-physician requirement obviously precludes therapeutic abortions from being performed in hospitals where four doctors are not available.

Moreover, the requirement in subs. 251(4) that lawful abortions can only be performed in "accredited" or "approved" hospitals also has the effect of contributing to the absence of hospitals, in some parts of Canada, in which lawful abortions are available. Subsection 251(6) defines "accredited hospital" as a hospital accredited by the Canadian Council on Hospital Accreditation in which diagnostic services and medical, surgical and obstetrical treatment are provided. Not only are there some hospitals unable to qualify because they do not provide all these services, but some hospitals also fail to meet the Council's accreditation requirements.

Alternatively, therapeutic abortions may be performed in hospitals "approved" by the Ministers of Health in the province, and standards to be met for approval vary considerably from province to province. The *Badgley Report*, at pp. 91 *et seq.*, noted this variation in 1977. In Newfoundland, for example, the Department of Health guidelines required hospitals seeking approval to establish therapeutic abortion committees to have a minimum of six members of the medical staff willing to cooperate with or recognize the existence of a therapeutic abortion committee, the presence of a gynaecologist on the medical staff, and 100 beds or more in the hospital, even though many abortions are done on an out-patient basis. Thus, of 46 public general hospitals in the province in 1976, 35 were excluded by these provincial criteria, leaving only 11 hospitals qualified to establish therapeutic abortion committees, with no obligation to do so. In Saskatchewan, where provincial regulations included a requirement of a rate bed capacity of 50 beds or more, 110 of 133 general hospitals were ineligible to establish a therapeutic abortion committee. In Ontario, where the provincial regulations included a requirement of ten or more members on a hospital's active medical staff, 51 of 205 general hospitals were ineligible to establish committees. The Criminal Code, under the "approved" hospital requirement, not only allows for an unequal distribution of hospitals across Canada, but also permits provincial authorities to set standards which appear at times largely irrelevant to the performance of therapeutic abortions.

Thus, the requirements of s. 251 seriously limit the number of hospitals which are eligible to perform lawful abortions, causing an absence or a serious lack of therapeutic abortion facilities in many parts of the country. The conclusions of the *Badgley Report* are startling:

> Of the total of 1,348 non-military hospitals in Canada in 1976, 789 hospitals, or 58.5 per cent, were ineligible in terms of their treatment functions, the size of their medical staff, or their type of facility to establish therapeutic abortion committees.
>
> (p. 105)

The rules in subs. 251(4) limiting the number of eligible hospitals means that a significant proportion of Canada's population is not served by hospitals in which therapeutic abortions can lawfully be performed. The *Badgley Report*, at p. 109, concluded in 1977 that 39.3 per cent of the total female population of Canada was not served by eligible hospitals. As we have already seen, the absence of eligible hospitals in some parts of Canada compels many pregnant women to leave their own communities to seek medical treatment in a place where an eligible hospital is available to admit them as patients. A pregnant woman in these circumstances will inevitably incur a delay in obtaining a therapeutic abortion.

The lack of hospitals with therapeutic abortion committees is made more serious by the refusal of certain hospital boards to appoint therapeutic abortion committees in hospitals which would otherwise qualify under the Criminal Code. Given that therapeutic abortions can only be performed in eligible hospitals and that the committee certifying the abortion must come from that hospital, this effectively contributes to the inaccessibility of the treatment. Nothing in the Criminal Code obliges the board of an eligible hospital to appoint therapeutic abortion committees. Indeed, a board is entitled to refuse to appoint a therapeutic abortion committee in a hospital that would otherwise qualify to perform abortions and boards often do so in Canada. Given that the decision to appoint a committee is, in part, one of conscience and, in some cases, one which affects religious beliefs, a law cannot force a board to appoint a committee any more than it could force a physician to perform an abortion. The defect in the law is not that it does not force boards to appoint committees, but that it grants exclusive authority to those boards to make such appointments.

In "Abortion and the Just Society" (1970), 5 R.J.T. 27 at 36, lawyer Natalie Fochs Isaacs correctly anticipated the effect of the exclusive authority of hospital boards in establishing committees:

> S. 237 [now s. 251] sets out the requirement of the certification of therapeutic abortion by a therapeutic abortion committee prior to its performance. But the section does not require any hospital to set up such a committee. Given the undesirability of forcing any hospital to do so, the restriction of legal abortions to this type of preliminary certification fails nevertheless to provide for alternative methods of prior medical consultation among those staff members of any hospital opposed to the creation of the committee required, who themselves approve of therapeutic abortions. The new legislation in this manner also places the prospective petitioner for the operation at the mercy of the institutional policy of what may be the only hospital available in her community.
>
> (Footnotes omitted.)

The *Badgley Report*, at p. 93, again documented the reduction of the number of hospitals with therapeutic abortion committees due to the refusal of boards of hospitals which would otherwise qualify under the law to appoint committees. In Newfoundland, six of the 11 hospitals which were otherwise qualified to perform therapeutic abortions did in fact appoint committees so that only six of a total of 46 general hospitals were eligible to perform therapeutic abortions under the Criminal Code. In Quebec, 31 of 128 general hospitals appointed therapeutic abortion committees. In Saskatchewan, 10 of 133 general hospitals appointed committees. In Manitoba, eight of 78 general hospitals appointed committees. Overall, the *Badgley Report*, *supra*, at 105, concluded in the following terms:

> In terms of all civilian hospitals (1,348) in Canada in 1976, 20.1 percent had established a therapeutic abortion committee. If only those general hospitals which met hospital practices and provincial requirements and were not exempt in terms of their special treatment facilities are considered, then of these 559 hospitals, 271 hospitals, or 48.5 percent, had established therapeutic abortion committees, while 288 hospitals, or 51.5 percent, did not have these committees.

According to the Powell Report, a comparable fraction of hospitals had established therapeutic abortion committees in Ontario: "out of 176 accredited acute care hospitals, 95 (54%) had therapeutic abortion committees" (at p. 24). The figures reported by the Badgley Committee in 1977 were confirmed in a recent Statistics Canada report according to which the total number of hospitals with therapeutic abortion committees fell across the country from 271 in 1976 to 250 in 1985 (Statistics Canada, *Therapeutic abortions 1985*, Ottawa, Supply and Services Canada: 1986 at 12).

For the purposes of the case at bar, it is important to reiterate that the absence of hospitals with therapeutic abortion committees in many parts of Canada is caused by the following requirements of the law:

(a) that a total of four physicians in the hospital must participate in the authorization and performance of the therapeutic abortion;

(b) that the hospital must be "approved" or "accredited"; and

(c) that only the board of the hospital is entitled to appoint a therapeutic abortion committee.

Finally, it is worth noting that 18% of the hospitals

that did have therapeutic abortion committees in 1984 performed no therapeutic abortions (Statistics Canada 1985, *supra*, at p. 38). Dr. Augustin Roy, the President of the Corporation professionnelle des médecins du Québec, testified at trial that of the 30 hospitals with therapeutic abortion committees in Quebec, "only about fourteen or fifteen of these hospitals are operational, because many of them, say half of them, have a committee but they don't do any abortions. It is a committee on paper."

A hospital with a dormant committee is no more useful to a pregnant woman seeking a therapeutic abortion than a hospital without a committee or no hospital at all. The delay suffered by a pregnant woman because her local hospital has a dormant committee is perhaps more the result of internal hospital policy than of s. 251 of the Criminal Code, but s. 251 is at least indirectly the cause of the delay in requiring an opinion from the therapeutic abortion committee of that hospital before a lawful abortion can be performed there.

(2) Delays caused by quotas

Delays result not only from the absence or inactivity of therapeutic abortion committees. The evidence discloses that some hospitals with committees impose quotas on the number of therapeutic abortions which they perform while others place quotas on patients depending on their place of residence. The evidence at trial confirmed that these quotas, initially observed in the *Badgley Report*, at pp. 258 *et seq.*, have been retained in many Canadian hospitals and that they often delay timely medical treatment for pregnant women seeking therapeutic abortions. It is true, of course, that these quotas are set by internal hospital policy and not by the terms of the law itself. It is also true that quotas may be necessary given hospitals' limited resources and the significant demands placed on those resources by pregnant women seeking abortions, some of whom may not qualify for therapeutic abortions in respect of the standard of subs. 251(4). There is evidence, however, of quotas in absolute numbers of abortions performed and quotas based on the place of residence which can affect women who otherwise qualify for lawful abortions under para. 251(4)(c). Indeed the Badgley Committee reported in 1977 that:

> Two out of five hospitals (38.2 percent) considered only applications from women who were considered to reside with the hospital's usual service catchment area. Residential requirements and patient quotas were more often adopted in the Maritimes (43.8 percent) and Quebec (66.7 percent) than among hospitals elsewhere where about a third followed this practice. Where the proportion of the hospitals with committees having these residency or quota requirements was higher in a province or a region, there were proportionately more women who went to the United States to obtain induced abortions.

> (*Supra*, at 259)

These quotas are inevitable given that s. 251 requires that therapeutic abortions be performed only in eligible hospitals and that there is a lack of hospitals with committees in some parts of the country. The quotas cannot, therefore, be said to reflect simple administrative or budgetary constraints. In this respect, the s. 251 procedure is again the source of delays in medical treatment.

(3) Delays caused by the committee requirement

The committee requirement itself contributes to a delay in securing treatment. The law requires the therapeutic abortion committee to certify that the standard of subs. 251(4) has been met before a therapeutic abortion can proceed lawfully. As I shall endeavour to explain in my consideration of s. 251 and the principles of fundamental justice, I believe that the state interest in the protection of the foetus justifies the requirement that the standard of subs. 251(4) be ascertained by independent medical opinion. This being the case, some delay will always be incurred whatever system is put in place to ensure that the standard has been met. However, at this stage of my analysis, I seek only to establish that a delay has in fact been caused by the present requirements of the Criminal Code.

The time needed to convene the committee in the hospital, for the pregnant woman's file to come before the committee, for her application to be evaluated by whatever means the committee may choose and for the certificate to be issued to the qualified medical practitioner together create some delay for obtaining treatment. The *Badgley Report*, at p. 146, identified an average interval of 8.0 weeks until the induced abortion operation was done *after* the pregnant woman's initial visit to her physician. Some of this delay is attributable to the absence of committees and hospital quotas which I have outlined above. It is difficult to isolate with precision the fraction of the delay attributable to the committee requirement taken by itself. It is relevant as one part of the overall delay which pregnant women must endure to obtain a therapeutic abortion.

In spite of evidence that the overall delay has been reduced, as will be seen shortly, the committee requirement continues to add to the delay. In 1987, the *Powell Report* identified as one problem the number of committee members who must certify that the subs. 251(4) standard has been met:

> The number of members on the TAC [therapeutic abortion committee] ranges from three to five although up to seven members sit on some committees. When five or seven members have been appointed and no quorum is stated, a majority of the committee (three to

five) must be present and three must approve each abortion. This has caused problems in several of the hospitals contacted, where it was not possible for an adequate number of members to be present and the meeting had to be rescheduled. Thus precious time was lost and the abortion delayed to a more advanced gestational age.

(At p. 27)

Furthermore, the delays caused by the committee requirements necessarily impact upon the pregnant woman who seeks to become a patient of the hospital for which the committee has been appointed. Paragraph 251(4)(*b*) states in part that it is "the therapeutic abortion committee *for that* accredited or approved hospital" which must issue the certificate (my emphasis). This precludes a committee from one hospital from authorizing abortions which take place at other hospitals. Eliminating such a requirement would have the effect of shortening the delays without forcing reluctant hospital boards or hospital staff to participate.

2. Consequences of the delays

The delays which a pregnant woman may have to suffer as a result of the requirements of subs. 251(4) must undermine the security of her person in order that there be a violation of this element of s. 7 of the Charter. As I said earlier, s. 7 cannot be invoked simply because a woman's pregnancy amounts to a medically dangerous condition. If, however, the delays occasioned by subs. 251(4) of the Criminal Code result in an additional danger to the pregnant woman's health, then the state has intervened and this intervention constitutes a violation of that woman's security of the person. By creating this additional risk, s. 251 prevents access to effective and timely medical treatment for the continued pregnancy which would or would be likely to endanger her life or health. If an effective and timely therapeutic abortion may only be obtained by committing a crime, then s. 251 violates the pregnant woman's right to security of the person.

The evidence reveals that delays caused by subs. 251(4) result in at least three broad types of additional medical risks. The risk of post-operative complications increases with delay. Secondly, there is a risk that the pregnant woman requires a more dangerous means of procuring a miscarriage because of the delay. Finally, since a pregnant woman knows her life or health is in danger, the delay caused by the subs. 251(4) procedure may result in an additional psychological trauma. I shall explain each of the additional risks in turn.

The Chief Justice outlined the different techniques employed to perform abortions at different stages of pregnancy and the increasing risk attached to each method as gestational age advances. As he also noted, the evidence showed that within the periods appropriate to each method of abortion, the earlier the abortion was performed, the lower the risk of complication. Evidence introduced at trial confirms findings in the *Badgley Report*, at pp. 308 *et seq.*, and the *Powell Report*, at p. 23, that the earlier an abortion is performed, the less chance a woman has of experiencing a post-operative complication, whatever abortion technique is used. The respondent agrees with this proposition but cites the low complication rate across Canada and the negligible mortality rate reported since 1974 as evidence that abortion under the current system is very safe. According to a 1985 Statistics Canada Report, *supra*, at p. 20, no Canadian women have died as a result of therapeutic abortion since 1979. One such death took place in 1974 and another in 1979.

It should be noted, however, that reported complication rates for any given abortion technique are generally limited to certain post-operative physical complications and do not include data on psychological complications inherent to those techniques. Furthermore, the psychological trauma that women suffer before the operation is not reflected in reported figures. This is equally true for any physical complications associated with the pregnant woman's initially dangerous condition which may arise during the delay before the therapeutic abortion.

However low the post-operative complication rate may appear, it *increases* as gestational age advances. In other words, with each passing week of pregnancy, even in the very early stages, the risk to health that an abortion represents increases. Statistics Canada information for 1982 confirms this. The complication rate for abortions performed under nine weeks was 0.7 per cent. This increased to 1.0 per cent in the 9 to 12 week gestation period. A complication rate of 8.5 per cent was reported for the 13 to 16 week gestation period. The complication rate for the 17 to 20 week gestation period was higher still, reported as 22 per cent (Statistics Canada, *Therapeutic abortions 1982*, Ottawa: Supply and Services Canada, 1984, at 111). Ontario statistics cited in the *Powell Report* confirm these national figures for that province. Data from 1976, 1981 and 1984 confirm the relation between abortion complications and gestational age in Ontario. In terms of absolute numbers, there were twice as many reported complications for women with gestational age 13 weeks and above compared to gestational age under 13 weeks. The rate expressed as a percentage of total reported therapeutic abortions performed ("per 100 gestational age specific abortions") was ten times higher for the group of women with gestational age 13 weeks and above (see *Powell Report*, at p. 23 and Table 4).

The procedure set forth in subs. 251(4) of the Criminal Code often causes, as we have seen, significant delays in obtaining therapeutic abortions. Delay increases the risk of post-operative complications. Subsection 251(4) thereby violates a pregnant woman's security of the person.

As I have already observed, the evidence indicates that the different techniques employed to perform abortions in Canada at different stages of pregnancy progressively increase risks to the woman. Expert testimony established that the suction dilation and curettage method generally used in the first twelve weeks is the safest technique. The dilation and evacuation method used from the thirteenth to the sixteenth week is relatively more dangerous. From the sixteenth week of pregnancy, an even more dangerous instillation method may be used. This method involves the introduction of prostaglandin, urea or saline solution which causes the woman to go into labour, giving birth to a foetus which is usually dead but not invariably so. Although the number of abortions done by the instillation technique amounts to only 4.5 per cent of the total number of therapeutic abortions performed in Canada, saline, urea or prostaglandin instillation is nevertheless used for 85.6 per cent of therapeutic abortions for women at least 16 weeks pregnant (Statistics Canada 1986, *supra*, at pp. 18 and 19). It has been shown that the complication rate increases dramatically with the use of the instillation procedure (*ibid* at 50). In addition, psychological trauma resulting from induced labour and the birth of the foetus is a very real consideration which is not included in post-operative statistics. It is in the pregnant woman's utmost interest that the delay for obtaining a therapeutic abortion be as short as possible so that the risks associated with more dangerous abortion techniques can be avoided.

Women are aware of the increased risk associated with the later stage abortion techniques. They are also aware of the more traumatic circumstances in which these techniques, particularly the instillation methods, are carried out. It is thus not only the risk of post-operative complications that increases progressively with each method. Women are aware of the increased risk well before the operation is performed. Experts testified at trial that awareness of the increased post-operative risk and of the added trauma associated with the later-stage methods create an increased psychological risk to health distinct from the increased physical risk. There is a world of difference, from the psychological point of view of the patient, between a reputedly safe technique of abortion performed under local anaesthetic requiring only a few hours in a hospital and an abortion procedure with a substantially higher complication rate performed under general anaesthetic requiring a longer period of hospitalization, and involving the trauma of induced labour and the delivery of a dead foetus. When the delays caused by subs. 251(4) require a woman to undergo a saline procedure abortion, for example, the psychological trauma associated with that procedure amounts to an additional risk to health attributable to the Criminal Code. More generally, the delay that a pregnant woman must endure before she receives treatment of any kind results in psychological trauma. To force a woman, under threat of criminal sanction, to wait for medical treatment when she knows that her pregnancy represents a danger to her life or health is a violation of her right to security of the person. As was stated in *Collin v. Lussier*, [1983] 1 F.C. 218 at 239 (later reversed on appeal [1985] 1 F.C. 124 but cited with approval on this point by Wilson J. in *Singh et al. v. Minister of Employment and Immigration*, [1985] 1 S.C.R. 178 at 208):

> . . . such detention, by increasing the applicant's anxiety as to his state of health, is likely to make his illness worse and, by depriving him of access to adequate medical care, it is in fact an impairment of the security of his person.

The psychological trauma that a pregnant woman suffers as a result of the delay shows that the procedure established by the Criminal Code violates the security of her person.

I have observed three instances in which s. 251 of the Criminal Code results in delays for women who qualify for therapeutic abortions in respect of the standard of para. 251(4)(c). This being said, the overall delay appears to have been reduced from the 8.0 weeks observed by the Badgley Committee in 1977. Evidence indicates that where a hospital with a committee is in place in a region, as in the case of Toronto, pregnant women can obtain therapeutic abortions within one to three weeks from their initial contact with a physician. Experts testified at trial that these delays are longer in some parts of the country, particularly in Quebec, but that overall delays have, on balance, been reduced. Furthermore, therapeutic abortion committees generally can speed up the certification process in an emergency situation, particularly when the pregnant woman's gestational age requires immediate medical attention. In spite of the reduction, however, these delays continue to result in an additional risk to the health of these women. The risk of post-operative complications increases with each passing week of delay. There is a heightened physical and psychological risk associated with later stage pregnancy techniques for abortion. Finally, psychological trauma increases with delay. The delays mean therefore that the state has intervened in such a manner as to create an additional risk to health, and consequently this intervention constitutes a violation of the woman's security of the person.

IV. The Principles of Fundamental Justice

I turn now to a consideration of the manner in which pregnant women are deprived of their right to security of the person by s. 251. Section 7 of the Charter states that everyone has the right not to be deprived of security of the person except in accordance with the principles of fundamental justice. As I will endeavour to demonstrate, subs. 251(4) does not accord with the principles of fundamental justice.

I am of the view, however, that certain elements of the procedure for obtaining a therapeutic abortion which counsel for the appellants argued could not be saved by the second part of s. 7 are in fact in accordance with the principles of fundamental justice. The expression of the standard in para. 251(4)(c), and the requirement for some independent medical opinion to ascertain that the standard has been met as well as the consequential necessity of some period of delay to ascertain the standard are not in breach of s. 7 of the Charter.

Counsel for the appellants argued that the expression of the standard in para. 251(4)(c) is so imprecise that it offends the principles of fundamental justice. He submits that pregnant women are arbitrarily deprived of their s. 7 right by reason of the different meanings that can be given to the word "health" in para. 251(4)(c) by therapeutic abortion committees.

I agree with Mr. Justice McIntyre and the Ontario Court of Appeal that the expression "the continuation of the pregnancy of such female person would or would be likely to endanger her life or health" found in para. 251(4)(c) does provide, as a matter of law, a sufficiently precise standard by which therapeutic abortion committees can determine when therapeutic abortions should be granted.

As the Court of Appeal said:

In this case . . . from a reading of s. 251 with its exceptions, there is no difficulty in determining what is proscribed and what is permitted. It cannot be said that no sensible meaning can be given to the words of the section. Thus, it is for the courts to say what meaning the statute will bear.

(*Supra*, at 387-8)

Chief Justice Laskin held in *Morgentaler (1975)* that para. 251(4)(*c*) was not so vague so as to constitute a violation of "security of the person" without due process of law under s. 1(*a*) of the Canadian Bill of Rights:

It is enough to say that Parliament has fixed a manageable standard because it is addressed to a professional panel, the members of which would be expected to bring a practised judgment to the question whether "the continuation of the pregnancy . . . would or would be like to endanger . . . life or health." Moreover, I am of the view that Parliament would assign such an exercise of judgment to a professional group without colliding with any imperatives called for by due process of law under s. 1(*a*).

(*Supra*, at 634)

I agree with Laskin C.J. that the standard is manageable because it is addressed to a panel of doctors exercising medical judgment on a medical question. This being the case, the standard must necessarily be flexible. Flexibility and vagueness are not synonymous. Parliament has set a medical standard to be determined over a limited range of circumstances. With the greatest of respect, I cannot agree with the view that the therapeutic abortion committee is a "strange hybrid, part medical committee and part legal committee" as the Chief Justice characterizes it. In subs. 251(4) Parliament has only given the committee the authority to make a medical determination regarding the pregnant woman's life or health. The committee is not called upon to evaluate the sufficiency of the state interest in the foetus as against the woman's health. This evaluation of the state interest is a question of law already decided by Parliament in its formulation of subs. 251(4). Evidence has been submitted that many committees fail to apply the standard set by Parliament by requiring the consent of the pregnant woman's spouse, by refusing to authorize second abortions or by refusing all abortions to married women. Insofar as these and other requirements fall outside para. 251(4)(c), they constitute an unfounded interpretation of the plain terms of the Criminal Code. These patent excesses of authority do not, however, mean that the standard of s. 251 is vague.

The wording of para. 251(4)(c) limits the authority of the committee. The word "health" is not vague but plainly refers to the physical or mental health of the pregnant woman. I note with interest the decision of the Supreme Court of the United States in *U.S. v. Vuitch*, 402 U.S. 62 (1971), in which a District of Columbia statute outlawing abortions except when they were "necessary for the preservation of the mother's life or health" was at issue. It was argued that the word "health" was so imprecise and had so uncertain a meaning that the statute offended the Due Process Clause of the United States Constitution. Mindful of the differences between the Due Process Clause and the principles of fundamental justice in s. 7 of the Charter, I nevertheless believe the following extract of the majority opinion delivered by Mr. Justice Black to be instructive:

> . . . the general usage and modern understanding of the word "health" . . . includes psychological as well as physical well-being. Indeed Webster's Dictionary, in accord with that common usage, properly defines health as the "[s]tate of being . . . sound in body [or] mind." Viewed in this light, the term "health" presents no problem of vagueness. Indeed, whether a particular

operation is necessary for a patient's physical or mental health is a judgment that physicians are obviously called upon to make routinely whenever surgery is considered.

(*Supra*, at 72)

The standard is further circumscribed by the word "endanger". Not only must the continuation of the pregnancy affect the woman's life or health, it must endanger life or health, so that a committee that authorizes an abortion when this element is not present or fails to authorize it when it is present exceeds its authority. Finally, the expression "would or would be likely" eliminates any requirement that the danger to life or health be certain or immediate at the time the certificate is issued.

The presence of the exculpatory provision in the Criminal Code and the wording of the standard itself point to the parameters of subs. 251(4). The required standard of threat to life or health must necessarily be lesser than that required under the common law defence of necessity, otherwise subs. 251(4) would be superfluous. It is proper to infer, on the other hand, that subs. 251(4) must be interpreted as relating solely to therapeutic grounds since only qualified medical practitioners are entitled to evaluate the threat to life or health.

Not only is the standard expressed in para. 251(4)(*c*) sufficiently precise to permit therapeutic abortion committees to determine when therapeutic abortions should be granted, but the crime of procuring a miscarriage is expressed with sufficient clarity for those subject to its terms so as not to offend the principles of fundamental justice. In this respect, counsel for the respondent correctly observed in his written argument that ". . . s. 251 presents no degree of uncertainty or vagueness as to potential criminal liability: anyone charged with an offence would know whether prohibited conduct was being undertaken and whether an exemption certificate had been received. Equally, any official entrusted with enforcing this section would know whether an offence had been committed." Police officers are not called upon by the section to define "health" but, in respect of the medical justification for a therapeutic abortion, they must ensure that a certificate in writing has been duly issued.

Just as the expression of the standard in para. 251(4)(*c*) does not offend the principles of fundamental justice, the requirement that an independent medical opinion be obtained for a therapeutic abortion to be lawful also cannot be said to constitute a violation of these principles when considered in the context of pregnant women's right to security of the person.

In *R. v. Jones*, [1986] 2 S.C.R. 284 at 304, La Forest J. explained that the legislator must be accorded a certain latitude to make choices regarding the type of administrative structure that will suit its needs unless the use of such structure is in itself "so manifestly unfair, *having regard to the decisions it is called upon to make* [my emphasis], as to violate the principles of *fundamental* justice". An administrative structure made up of unnecessary rules, which result in an additional risk to the health of pregnant women, is manifestly unfair and does not conform to the principles of fundamental justice. Subsection 251(4), taken as a whole, does not accord with the principles of fundamental justice in that certain of the procedural requirements of s. 251 create unnecessary delays. As will be seen, some of these requirements are manifestly unfair because they have no connection whatsoever with Parliament's objectives in establishing the administrative structure in subs. 251(4). Although connected to Parliament's objectives, other rules in subs. 251(4) are manifestly unfair because they are not necessary to assure that the objectives are met.

As I noted in my analysis of subs. 251(4), by requiring that a committee state that the medical standard has been met for the criminal sanction to be lifted, Parliament seeks to assure that there is a reliable, independent and medically sound opinion that the continuation of the pregnancy would or would be likely to endanger the woman's life or health. Whatever the failings of the current system, I believe that the purpose pursuant to which it was adopted does not offend the principles of fundamental justice. As I shall endeavour to explain, the current mechanism in the Criminal Code does not accord with the principles of fundamental justice. This does not preclude, in my view, Parliament from adopting another system, free of the failings of subs. 251(4), in order to ascertain that the life or health of the pregnant woman is in danger, by way of a reliable, independent and medically sound opinion.

Parliament is justified in requiring a reliable, independent and medically sound opinion in order to protect the state interest in the foetus. This is undoubtedly the objective of a rule which requires an independent verification of the practising physician's opinion that the life or health of the pregnant woman is in danger. It cannot be said to be simply a mechanism designed to protect the health of the pregnant woman. While this latter objective clearly explains the requirement that the practising physician be a "qualified medical practitioner" and that the abortion take place in a safe place, it cannot explain the necessary intercession of an in-hospital committee of three physicians from which is excluded the practising physician.

While a second medical opinion is very often seen as necessary in medical circles when difficult questions as to a patient's life or health are at issue, the independent opinion called for by the Criminal Code has a different purpose. Parliament requires this independent opinion because it is not only the woman's interest that is at stake in a decision to authorize an abortion. The Ontario Court of Appeal alluded to this at pp. 377-78 when it stated that "[o]ne cannot overlook the fact that the situation respecting a woman's right to control her own person becomes more complex when she becomes pregnant and that some statutory control may be appropriate". The presence of the foetus accounts for this complexity. By requiring an independent medical opinion that the pregnant woman's life or health is in fact endangered, Parliament seeks to ensure that, in any given case, only therapeutic reasons will justify the decision to abort. The amendments to the Criminal Code in 1969 amounted to a recognition by Parliament, as I have said, that the interest in the life or health of the pregnant woman takes precedence over the interest of the state in the protection of the foetus when the continuation of the pregnancy would or would be likely to endanger the pregnant woman's life or health. Parliament decided that it was necessary to ascertain this from a medical point of view before the law would allow the interest of the pregnant woman to indeed take precedence over that of the foetus and permit an abortion to be performed without criminal sanction.

I do not believe it to be unreasonable to seek independent medical confirmation of the threat to the woman's life or health when such an important and distinct interest hangs in the balance. I note with interest that in a number of foreign jurisidictions, laws which decriminalize abortions require an opinion as to the state of health of the woman independent from the opinion of her own physician. The Crown, in its book of authorities, cited the following statutes which included such a mechanism: United Kingdom, Abortion Act, 1967, c. 87, s. 1(1)(a); Australian Northern Territory, Criminal Law Consolidation Act, s. 79 A(3)(a); South Australia, Criminal Law Consolidation Act, 1935-1975, s. 82a(1)(a); West Germany, Criminal Code, as amended by the Fifteenth Criminal Law Amendment Act (1976), s. 219; Israel, Penal Law, 5737-1977 (as amended), s. 315; New Zealand, Crimes Act 1961, as amended by the Crimes Amendment Act 1977 and the Crimes Amendment Act 1978, s. 187A(4); Code pénal suisse, art. 120(1). This said, the practising physician must, according to para. 251(4)(*a*), be in "good faith" and, consequently, have no reason to believe that the standard in para. 251(4)(*c*) has not been met. The practising physician is, however, properly excluded from the body giving the independent opinion. I believe that Parliament is justified in requiring what is no doubt an extraordinary medical practice in its regulation of the criminal law of abortion in accordance with the various interests at stake.

The assertion that an independent medical opinion, distinct from that of the pregnant woman and her practising physician, does not offend the principles of fundamental justice would need to be reevaluated if a right of access to abortion is founded upon the right to "liberty" in s. 7 of the Charter. I am of the view that there would still be circumstances in which the state interest in the protection of the foetus would require an independent medical opinion as to the danger to the life or health of the pregnant woman. Assuming without deciding that a right of access to abortion can be founded upon the right to "liberty", there would be a point in time at which the state interest in the foetus would become compelling. From this point in time, Parliament would be entitled to limit abortions to those required by therapeutic reasons and therefore require an independent opinion as to the health exception. The case law reveals a substantial difference of opinion as to the state interest in the protection of the foetus as against the pregnant woman's right to liberty. Madame Justice Wilson, for example, in her discussion of s. 1 of the Charter in the case at bar, notes the following:

The precise point in the development of the foetus at which the state's interest in its protection becomes "compelling" I leave to the informed judgment of the legislature which is in a position to receive guidance on the subject from all the relevant disciplines. It seems to me, however, that it would fall somewhere in the second trimester.

This view as to when the state interest becomes compelling may be compared with that of Justice O'Connor of the United States Supreme Court in her dissenting opinion in *City of Akron v. Akron Center for Reproductive Health, Inc.*, 103 S.Ct. 2481 at 2509 (1983):

> In *Roe* [*Roe v. Wade* 410 U.S. 113 (1973)], the Court held that although the State had an important and legitimate interest in protecting potential life, that interest could not become compelling until the point at which the fetus was viable. The difficulty with this analysis is clear: *potential* life is no less potential in the first weeks of pregnancy than it is at viability or afterward. At any stage in pregnancy, there is the *potential* for human life. Although the Court refused to "resolve the difficult question of when life begins", *id.*, 410 U.S. at 159, 93, S.Ct., at 730, the Court chose the point of viability — when the foetus is *capable* of life independent of its mother — to permit the complete proscription of abortion. The choice of viability as the point at which state interest in *potential* life becomes compelling is no less arbitrary than choosing any point before viability or any point afterward. Accordingly, I believe that the State's interest in protecting potential human life exists throughout the pregnancy.

As I indicated at the outset of my reasons, it is nevertheless possible to resolve this appeal without attempting to delineate the right to "liberty" in s. 7 of the Charter. The violation of the right to "security of the person" and the relevant principles of fundamental justice are sufficient to invalidate s. 251 of the Criminal Code. Some delay is inevitable in connection with any system which purports to limit to therapeutic reasons the grounds upon which an abortion can be performed lawfully. Any statutory mechanism for ensuring an independent confirmation as to the state of the woman's life or health, adopted pursuant to the objective of assuring the protection of the foetus, will inevitably result in a delay which would exceed whatever delay would be encountered if an independent opinion was not required. Furthermore, rules promoting the safety of abortions designed to protect the interest of the pregnant woman will also cause some unavoidable delay. It is only insofar as the administrative structure creates delays which are unnecessary that the structure can be considered to violate the principles of fundamental justice. Indeed, an examination of the delays caused by certain of the procedural requirements in subs. 251(4) reveals that they are unnecessary, given Parliament's objectives in establishing the administrative structure. I note parenthetically that it is not sufficient to argue that the structure would operate in a fair manner but for the applications from women who do not qualify in respect of the standard in para. 251(4)(c). A fair structure, put in place to decide between those women who qualify for a therapeutic abortion and those who do not, should be designed with a view to efficiently meeting the demands which it must necessarily serve.

One such example of a rule which is unnecessary is the requirement in subs. 251(4) that therapeutic abortions must take place in an eligible hospital to be lawful. I have observed that subs. 251(4) directs that therapeutic abortions take place in accredited or approved hospitals, with at least four physicians, and that, because of the lack of such hospitals in many parts of Canada, this often causes delay for women seeking treatment. As I noted earlier, this requirement was plainly adopted to assure the safety of the abortion procedure generally, and particularly the safety of the pregnant woman, *after* the standard of subs. 251(4) has been met and *after* the certificate to this effect has been issued enabling the woman to have a lawful abortion. The objective in respect of which the in-hospital rule was adopted is safety and not the state interest in the protection of the foetus. As the rule stands in subs. 251(4), however, no exception is currently possible. The evidence discloses that there is no justification for the requirement that all therapeutic abortions take place in hospitals eligible under the Criminal Code. In this sense, the delays which result from the hospital requirement are unnecessary and, consequently, in this respect, the administrative structure for therapeutic abortions is manifestly unfair and offends the principles of fundamental justice.

Experts testified at trial that the principal justification for the in-hospital rule is the problem of post-operative complications. There are of course instances in which the danger to life or health observed by the therapeutic abortion committee will constitute sufficient grounds for the procedure to take place in a hospital. There are other instances in which the circumstances of the procedure itself requires that it be performed in hospital, such as certain abortions performed at an advanced gestational age or cases in which the patient is particularly vulnerable to what might otherwise be a simple procedure.

In many cases, however, there is no medical justification that the therapeutic abortion take place in a hospital. Experts testified at trial, that many first trimester therapeutic abortions may be safely performed in specialized clinics outside of hospitals because the possible complications can be handled, and in some cases better handled, by the facilities of a specialized clinic. The parties submitted statistics comparing complication rates for in-hospital abortions and those performed in non-hospital facilities. These statistics are of limited value for our purposes because, not surprisingly, the higher reported rates in hospitals are due in part to the fact that the more dangerous cases are treated in hospital. What is more revealing, however, are statistics which show that a high percentage of therapeutic abortions performed in Canada are performed on an out-patient basis:

> The average length of stay in hospitals per therapeutic abortion case was less than a day in 1985. This average includes 46,567 cases or 76.9% of 60,518 therapeutic abortion cases for women, for whom the pregnancy terminations took place on an outpatient (day care) basis. The per cent of outpatient therapeutic abortions increased to 76.9% in 1985 from 59.7% in 1981 and 34.9% in 1975.

> (Statistics Canada 1985, *supra*, at p. 20)

The substantial increase in the percentage of abortions performed on an out-patient basis since 1975 underscores the view that the in-hospital requirement, which may have been justified when it was first adopted, has become exorbitant. One suspects that the number of out-patient abortions would be even higher if the Criminal Code did not prevent women in many parts of Canada from obtaining timely and effective treatment by requiring them to travel to places where eligible hospital facilities were available. Furthermore, these figures do not include out-patient abortions which may have qualified as therapeutic under the standard in para. 251(4)(c) which were performed on Canadian women in the United States and in clinics currently operating in Canada outside the subs. 251(4) exception. Citing the Canadian abortion law's in-hospital requirement as a legislative standard which is difficult to satisfy, Rebecca J. Cook and Bernard Dickens observe that "[r]igid statutory formulae may not improve . . . distribution of services but may obstruct appropriate response to health needs": *Abortion Laws in Commonwealth Countries* (Granchamp, France: World Health Organization, 1979), at p. 28.

In the *Powell Report*, several recommendations were made as to options for abortion service delivery in Ontario. In support of these recommendations, the *Report* included the following:

> When many countries legalized abortion, hospitals were viewed as the appropriate providers of safe abortion services. Since then, studies have demonstrated that abortions can be performed safely in other types of facilities (Tietze & Henshaw, 1986). The complication rate for all abortions performed in nonhospital facilities is no higher than for those which take place in hospitals (Grimes *et al.*, 1981)....
>
> Hospitals are often hard pressed to find time in the busy operating room schedules to fit in abortion procedures. In most hospitals, abortions are not viewed as a priority for scheduling. Gynaecologists must fit abortions into their allotted time in operating rooms. Although abortions can be performed in minor procedure rooms with no jeopardy to the patient, this is an unusual practice.
>
> (*Supra*, at pp. 21 and 35)

The presence of legislation in other jurisdictions permitting certain abortions to be performed outside of hospitals is especially revealing as to the safety of the procedure in those circumstances and of the necessity to provide alternative means given the limited resources of hospitals. In the *Powell Report*, it was observed that:

> In a number of European countries, including the Netherlands, Poland and West Germany, approximately half of the abortions are performed in nonhospital facilities. In France in 1982, 53 percent of abortions were performed in 90 "centres d'interruption volontaire de grossesse" which were administered by hospitals but were in practice separate abortion clinics.

The French government ordered all public hospitals that could not meet the demand for abortions to provide such clinics.

(*Supra*, at p. 21)

Particularly striking is the United States experience in respect of the in-hospital rule. The *Powell Report* noted that 82 per cent of abortions performed in the United States in 1982 were done outside of hospitals (*supra*, at p. 22). Experts confirmed this finding at trial. Dr. Christopher Tietze, a recognized expert on abortion, explained at trial that in 1981 all out-of-hospital abortion clinics in the United States performed abortions up to 10 weeks gestational age, 90 per cent of clinics performed abortions up to 12 weeks, 50 per cent of clinics up to 14 weeks and 20 per cent accepted patients up to 16 weeks. Although the legal basis upon which women assert a constitutional right of access to abortion is different in the United States than that which I find in the case at bar, the American experience as to the inappropriateness of a universal in-hospital requirement remains relevant.

The *Powell Report* proposed a number of projects as alternatives to the in-hospital rule for therapeutic abortions. Each proposal is designed to be "under the jurisdiction of a hospital board or several hospital boards with approval for abortion services provided through hospital therapeutic abortion committee mechanisms" (*supra*, at p. 37). One such proposal is for the establishment of comprehensive women's health care clinics which would provide first trimester abortions, referrals to hospitals for second trimester abortions and post-abortion counselling. Regional centres for therapeutic abortion clinics affiliated with but not necessarily located in a hospital are also proposed in the *Report*, which goes on to emphasize that first trimester ambulatory abortions are those most appropriate for a non-hospital setting.

The Badgley Committee also made a series of proposals designed to reduce the number and type of complications associated with therapeutic abortions. These included a proposal for "concentrating the performance of the abortion procedure into specialized units with a full range of the required equipment and facilities and staffed by experienced and specially trained nurses and medical personnel" (*supra*, at p. 322).

Whatever the eventual solution may be, it is plain that the in-hospital requirement is not justified in all cases. Although the protection of health of the woman is the objective which the in-hospital rule is intended to serve, the requirement that all therapeutic abortions be performed in eligible hospitals is unnecessary to meet that objective in all cases. In this sense, the rule is manifestly unfair and offends the principles of fundamental justice. I appreciate that the precise nature of the administrative solution may be complicated by the constitutional division of powers between Parliament and the provinces. There is no doubt that Parliament could allow the criminal law exception to operate in all hospitals, for example, though the provinces retain the power to establish these hospitals under s. 92(7) of the Constitution Act, 1867. On the other hand, if Parliament decided to allow therapeutic abortions to be performed in provincially licensed clinics, it is possible that both Parliament and the provinces would be called upon to collaborate in the implementation of the plan.

An objection can also be raised in respect of the requirement that the committee come from the accredited or approved hospital in which the abortion is to be performed. It is difficult to see a connection between this requirement and any of the practical purposes for which subs. 251(4) was enacted. It cannot be said to have been adopted in order to promote the safety of therapeutic abortions or the safety of the pregnant woman. Nor is the rule designed to preserve the state interest in the foetus. The integrity of the independent medical opinion is no better served by a committee within the hospital than a committee from outside the hospital as long as the practising physician remains excluded in both circumstances as part of a proper state participation in the choice of the procedure necessary to secure an independent opinion.

In a recent unpublished paper entitled *Options for Abortion Policy Reform: A Consultation Document* (Ottawa: unpublished, September 1986) at p. 74, the Fetal Status Working Group (Edward W. Keyserlingk, Director), Protection of Life Project of the Law Reform Commission of Canada confirmed the view that the requirement that abortion committees be limited to hospitals is unnecessary:

> Restricting the existence of these committees to hospitals appears to be one of the reasons for delays and inequitable access. There appears to be no compelling medical reason why committees should not be attached to clinics which are equipped and licensed to provide this procedure.

The Law Reform Commission's Working Group raises the possibility of regional abortion committees to replace the current rule (*supra*, at p. 76). The Powell Report proposals include a model whereby a central therapeutic abortion committee could serve several hospitals (*supra*, at p. 38).

Whatever solution is finally retained, it is plain that the requirement that the therapeutic abortion committee come from the hospital in which the abortion will be performed serves no real purpose. The risk resulting from the delay caused by subs. 251(4) in this respect is unnecessary. Consequently, this requirement violates the principles of fundamental justice.

Other aspects of the committee requirement in subs. 251(4) add to the manifest unfairness of the administrative structure. These include requirements which are at best only tenuously connected to the purpose of obtaining independent confirmation that the standard in para. 251(4)(c) has been met and which do not usefully contribute to the realization of that purpose. Hospital boards are entitled to appoint committees made up of three or more qualified medical practitioners. As I observed earlier, if more than three members are appointed, precious time can be lost when quorum cannot be established because members are absent. Whatever the number of members necessary to arrive at an independent appreciation of the state of the woman's life or health may in fact be, this number should be kept to the minimum to avoid unnecessary delays which, as I have explained, result in increased risk to women. Allowing a board to increase the number of members above a statutory minimum of three members does not add to the integrity of the independent opinion. This aspect of the current rule is unnecessary and, since it can result in increased risks, offends the principles of fundamental justice.

Similarly, the exclusion of all physicians who practise therapeutic abortions from the committees is exorbitant. This rule was no doubt included in subs. 251(4) to promote the independence of the therapeutic abortion committees' appreciation of the standard. As I have said, the exclusion of the practising physician, although it diverges from usual medical practice, is appropriate in the criminal context to ensure the independent opinion with respect to the life or health of that physician's patient. The exclusion of all physicians who perform therapeutic abortions from committees, even when they have no connection with the patient in question, is not only unnecessary but potentially counterproductive. There are no reasonable grounds to suspect bias from a physician who has no connection with the patient simply because, in the course of his or her medical practice, he or she performs *lawful* abortions. Furthermore, physicians who perform therapeutic abortions have useful expertise which would add to the precision and the integrity of the independent opinion itself. Some state control is appropriate to ensure the independence of the opinion. However, this rule as it now stands is excessive and can increase the risk of delay because fewer physicians are qualified to serve on the committees.

The foregoing analysis of the administrative structure of subs. 251(4) is by no means a complete catalogue of all the current systems' strengths and failings. It demonstrates, however, that the administrative structure put in place by Parliament has enough shortcomings so that subs. 251(4), when considered as a whole, violates the principles of fundamental justice. These shortcomings stem from rules which are not necessary to the purposes for which subs. 251(4) was established. These unnecessary rules, because they impose delays which result in an additional risk to women's health, are manifestly unfair.

V. Section 1 of the Charter

I agree with the view that s. 1 of the Charter can be used to save a legislative provision which breaches s. 7 in the manner which s. 251 of the Criminal Code violates s. 7 in this case. Section 1 states:

> 1. The Canadian Charter of Rights and Freedoms guarantees the rights and freedoms set out in it subject

108

only to such reasonable limits prescribed by law as can be demonstrably justified in a free and democratic society.

The Chief Justice provided an analysis of s. 1 in *R. v. Oakes*, [1986] 1 S.C.R. 103 at pp. 138-139 which is appropriate for the purposes of addressing s. 1 in the case at bar. Those seeking to uphold s. 251 of the Criminal Code must demonstrate the following:

> (1) the objective which s. 251 is designed to serve must "relate to concerns which are pressing and substantial"; and
> (2) "once a sufficiently significant objective is recognized then the party invoking s. 1 must show that the means chosen are reasonable and demonstrably justified. This involves a 'form of proportionality test'."

I shall also consider each of these criteria which must be met if the limit on the s. 7 right is to be found reasonable.

(1) The objective of s. 251

I agree with Madame Justice Wilson's characterization of s. 251, explained in the following terms:

> In my view, the primary objective of the impugned legislation must be seen as the protection of the foetus. It undoubtedly has other ancillary objectives, such as the protection of the life and health of pregnant women, but I believe that the main objective advanced to justify a restriction on the pregnant woman's s. 7 right is the protection of the foetus.

The primary objective of the protection of the foetus is the main objective relevant to the analysis of s. 251 under the first test of *Oakes*. With the greatest respect, I believe the Chief Justice incorrectly identifies the objective of *balancing* foetal interests and those of pregnant women, "with the lives and health of women as a major factor", as "sufficiently important to meet the requirements of the first step of the *Oakes* inquiry under s. 1".

The focus in *Oakes* is the objective "which the measures responsible for a limit on a Charter right or freedom are designed to serve" (*supra*, at p. 138). In the context of the criminal law of abortion, the objective which the measures in s. 251 responsible for a limit on the s. 7 Charter right are designed to serve is the protection of the foetus. The narrow aim of subs. 251(4) should not be confused with the primary objective of s. 251 as a whole. Given that s. 251 is a "comprehensive code", to use the expression of the Chief Justice, it is inappropriate, in my view, to focus on the exculpatory provision alone as the statement of Parliament's objective in establishing the crime. (See *R. v. Edwards Books*, [1986] 2 S.C.R. 713 at 751, in which the Court unanimously held that an exemption must be read in light of the affirmative provision to which it relates.) The ancillary objective of protecting the life or health of the pregnant woman, whether viewed alone or balanced against the protection of the foetus, is not the primary objective which the measures responsible for a limit on the constitutional right to security of the person were put in place to achieve.

This balance cannot be considered as Parliament's objective in establishing the crime nor in maintaining this activity as a crime following the amendments to the Criminal Code in 1969. Subsection 251(4) only applies in specified circumstances. When the life or health of a pregnant woman is not in danger and she seeks an abortion on the basis of her own non-medical "priorities and aspirations", it is plain that the rules in s. 251 precluding her from obtaining a lawful abortion have as their sole objective the protection of the foetus.

Furthermore, as federal legislation in respect of Parliament's jurisdiction over the criminal law in s.

91(27) of the Constitution Act, 1867, s. 251 cannot be said to have as its sole or principle objective, as the appellants argue, the protection of the life or health of pregnant women. Legislation which in its pith and substance is related to the life or health of pregnant women, depending of course on its precise terms, would be characterized as in relation to one of the provincial heads of power (see *Schneider v. The Queen*, [1982] 2 S.C.R. 112 at 137 *per* Dickson J., as he then was). The exculpatory provision in subs. 251(4) cannot stand on its own as a valid exercise of Parliament's criminal law power.

Does the objective of protecting the foetus in s. 251 relate to concerns which are pressing and substantial in a free and democratic society? The answer to the first step of the *Oakes* test is yes. I am of the view that the protection of the foetus is and, as the Court of Appeal observed, always has been, a valid objective in Canadian criminal law. I have already elaborated on this objective in my discussion of the principles of fundamental justice. I think s. 1 of the Charter authorizes reasonable limits to be put on a woman's right having regard to the state interest in the protection of the foetus.

(2) Proportionality

I turn now to the second test in *Oakes*. The Crown must show that the means chosen in s. 251 are reasonable and demonstrably justified. In *Oakes*, *supra*, at p. 139, the Chief Justice outlined three components of the proportionality test:

> First, the measures adopted must be carefully designed to achieve the objective in question. They must not be arbitrary, unfair or based on irrational considerations. In short, they must be rationally connected to the objective. Second, the means, even if rationally connected to the objective in this first sense, should impair "as little as possible" the right or freedom in question: *R. v.*

Big M Drug Mart Ltd., . . . at p. 352. Third, there must be a proportionality between the *effects* of the measures which are responsible for limiting the *Charter* right or freedom, and the objective which has been identified as of "sufficient importance".

For the purposes of the first component of proportionality, I observe that it was necessary, in my discussion of subs. 251(4) and the principles of fundamental justice, to explain my view that certain of the roles governing access to therapeutic abortions free from criminal sanction are unnecessary in respect of the objectives which s. 251 is designed to serve. A rule which is unnecessary in respect of Parliament's objectives cannot be said to be "rationally connected" thereto or to be "carefully designed to achieve the objective in question". Furthermore, not only are some of the rules in s. 251 unnecessary to the primary objective of the protection of the foetus and the ancillary objective of the protection of the pregnant woman's life or health, but their practical effect is to undermine the health of the woman which Parliament purports to consider so important. Consequently, s. 251 does not meet the proportionality test in Oakes.

There is no saving s. 251 by simply severing the offending portions of subs. 251(4). The current rule expressed in s. 251, which articulates both Parliament's principal and ancillary objectives, cannot stand without the exception in subs. 251(4). The violation of pregnant women's security of the person would be greater, not lesser, if subs. 251(4) was severed leaving the remaining subsections of s. 251 as they are in the Criminal Code.

Given my conclusion in respect of the first component of the proportionality test, it is not necessary to address the questions as to whether the means in s. 251 "impair as little as possible" the s. 7 Charter right and whether there is a proportionality between the effects of

s. 251 and the objective of protecting the foetus. Thus, I am not required to answer the difficult question concerning the circumstances in which there is a proportionality between the effects of s. 251 which limit the right of pregnant women to security of the person and the objective of the protection of the foetus. I do feel bound, however, to comment upon the balance which Parliament sought to achieve between the interest in the protection of the foetus and the interest in the life or health of the pregnant woman in adopting the amendments to the Criminal Code in 1969.

In *Oakes, supra,* at 140, the Chief Justice further explained the third component of the proportionality test in the following terms:

> Even if an objective is of sufficient importance, and the first two elements of the proportionality test are satisfied, it is still possible that, because of the *severity* of the deleterious effects of a measure on individuals or groups, the measure will not be justified by the purposes it is intended to serve. The more severe the deleterious effects of a measure, the more important the objective must be if the measure is to be reasonable and demonstrably justified in a free and democratic society. (My emphasis.)

The objective of protecting the foetus would not justify, in my view, the severity of the breach of pregnant women's right to security which would result if the exculpatory provision was completely removed from the Criminal Code.

The gist of subs. 251(4) is, as I have said, that the objective of protecting the foetus is not of sufficient importance to defeat the interest in protecting pregnant women from pregnancies which represent a danger to life or health. I take this parliamentary enactment in 1969 as an indication that, in a free and democratic society, it would be unreasonable to limit the pregnant woman's right to security of the person by a rule prohibiting abortions in all circumstances when her life or health would or would likely be in danger. This decision of the Canadian Parliament to the effect that the life or health of the pregnant woman takes precedence over the state interest in the foetus is also reflected in legislation in other free and democratic societies.

In *Emerging Issues in Commonwealth Abortion Laws, 1982* (London: Commonwealth Secretariat, 1983) *passim*, submitted as an exhibit at trial, Rebecca J. Cook and Bernard Dickens report that, on the basis of the law in force as of November 1, 1982, the United Kingdom, New Zealand and Australia Capital Territory, New South Wales, Northern Territory, Queensland, South Australia, and Victoria, among other Commonwealth jurisdictions, include risk to the pregnant woman's life, physical health and mental health as legal grounds for abortion. The Crown and the Attorney General of Canada, in their books of authorities, cited statutes from these and other jurisdictions which indicate that a danger to the life or health of the pregnant woman takes precedence over the state interest in the foetus: the United Kingdom, Abortion Act, 1967, c. 87, s. 1(1)(*a*); Australian Northern Territory, Criminal Law Consolidation Act and Ordinance, s. 79A(3)(*a*); South Australia, Criminal Law Consolidation Act 1935-1975, s. 82a(1)(*a*)(*i*); West Germany, Criminal Code, as amended by the Fifteenth Criminal Law Amendment Act (1976), s. 218a(1); Israel, Penal Law, 5737-1977 (as amended), art. 316(*a*)(4); New Zealand, Crimes Act 1961, as amended by the Crimes Amendment Act 1977 and the Crimes Amendment Act 1978, s. 187A(1)(*a*); and France, Code pénal, art. 317 and Code de la santé publique, art. 162-1 and 162-12. This substantiates the view that the legislative decision in Canada that the life or health of the woman takes precedence over the state interest in the foetus is in accordance with s. 1 of the Charter.

I note that the laws in some of these foreign jurisdictions, unlike s. 251 of the Criminal Code, require a higher standard of danger to health in the latter months of pregnancy, as opposed to the early months, for an abortion to be lawful. Would such a rule, if it was adopted in Canada, constitute a reasonable limit on the right to security of the person under s. 1 of the Charter? As I have said, given the actual wording of s. 251, pursuant to which the standard necessary for a lawful abortion does not vary according to the stage of pregnancy, this Court is not required to consider this question under s. 1 of the Charter. It is possible that a future enactment by Parliament along the lines of the laws adopted in these jurisdictions could achieve a proportionality which is acceptable under s. 1. As I have stated, however, I am of the view that the objective of protecting the foetus would not justify the complete removal of the exculpatory provisions from the Criminal Code.

Finally, I wish to stress that we have not been asked to decide nor is it necessary, given my own conclusion that s. 251 contains rules unnecessary to the protection of the foetus, to decide whether a foetus is included in the word "everyone" in s. 7 so as to have a right to "life, liberty and security of the person" under the Charter.

VI. Other Grounds for Appeal

Counsel for appellants raised several other grounds for appeal before this Court. The argument concerning the alleged invalidity of para. 605(1)(a) of the Criminal Code is the only Charter argument, apart from that pertaining to s. 7, which must be addressed. If the Crown had no right of appeal, the appellants woul⌐

necessarily succeed on this sole ground as this Court would be required to quash the decision of the Court of Appeal. Although, as a result of my answers to the first and second constitutional questions, I am not required to respond to the other arguments to dispose of this appeal, I believe that it is appropriate to answer the non-Charter issues.

Section 91(27) of the Constitution Act, 1867

I agree with McIntyre J. and the Court of Appeal that there is no merit in the argument that s. 251 is *ultra vires* of Parliament. In *Morgentaler (1975), supra,* this Court unanimously held that s. 251 is not colourable provincial legislation in relation to health but that it constitutes a proper exercise of Parliament's criminal law power pursuant to s. 91(27) of the Constitution Act, 1867. I agree. Indeed, as I have decided, s. 251 cannot be said to be simply a mechanism designed to protect the life or health of the pregnant woman. While this ancillary objective explains, in part, certain of the requirements of the exculpatory provision in subs. 251(4), it does not represent the principal objective of s. 251 as a whole, which is to protect the state interest in the foetus. Parliament established the indictable offence of procuring a miscarriage, defined in subs. 251(1) and subs. 251(2), pursuant to this primary objective. I consider this a valid exercise of the criminal law power.

Section 96 of the Constitution Act, 1867

I agree with McIntyre J. that s. 251 does not give judicial powers to therapeutic abortion committees which were exercised by country, district and superior courts at the time of Confederation. As I have observed, in subs. 251(4) Parliament has only given the committee the authority to make a medical determination regarding the pregnant woman's life or health. The panel of doctors exercises medical judgment on a medical question and performs no s. 96 judicial function. There is no merit in this argument.

Unlawful Delegation and Abdication of the Criminal Law Power

For the reasons given by McIntyre J., I agree that s. 251 does not constitute an unlawful delegation of federal legislative power nor does it represent an abdication of the criminal law power by Parliament.

Paragraph 605(1)(a) of the Criminal Code

For the reasons given by McIntyre J., I agree that there is no merit in this argument.

Subsection 610(3) of the Criminal Code

Counsel for the appellants argued that subs. 610(3) of the Criminal Code, which prohibits the awarding of costs in appeals involving indictable offences, violates ss. 7, 11(*d*), 11(*f*), 11(*h*) and 15 of the Charter. He also argued that this Court had the power to award costs on appeals under s. 24(1) of the Charter. It is unnecessary to decide whether or not subs. 610(3) of the Criminal Code violates a Charter right. I agree with the Court of Appeal that whatever this Court's power to award costs in appeals such as this one, costs should not be awarded in this case.

* * *

With regard to defence counsel's address to the jury at trial, I associate myself completely with the comments made by the Chief Justice. In his address, Mr. Manning wrongly chose not to respect the very distinct roles the trial judge and the jury play in our system of criminal justice. In *R. v. Mezzo*, [1986] 1 S.C.R. 802, at p. 836, McIntyre J., in a different context, stated:

No authority need be cited for the proposition that in a jury trial all questions of law are for the judge alone and, of equal importance, all questions of fact are for the jury alone. The distinction is of fundamental importance. It should be preserved so long as it is considered right to continue the use of the jury in criminal law.

The defence submission was, as the Court of Appeal stated, "a direct attack on the role and authority of the trail judge and a serious misstatement to the jury as to its duty and right in carrying out its oath" (*supra*, at p. 434). I am of the view that these strongly-stated observations are required for the benefit of counsel who in other proceedings may be tempted to follow this unacceptable practice.

Conclusion

The constitutional questions should be answered as follows:

1. **Question:**
   Does section 251 of the Criminal Code of Canada infringe or deny the rights and freedoms guaranteed by sections 2(a), 7, 12, 15, 27 and 28 of the Canadian Charter of Rights and Freedoms?
   Answer:
   The first constitutional question is answered in the affirmative in respect of the right of a pregnant woman to "security of the person" in s. 7 of the Charter.

2. **Question:**
   If section 251 of the Criminal Code of Canada infringes or denies the rights and freedoms guaranteed by sections 2(a), 7, 12, 15, 27 and 28 of the Canadian Charter of Rights and Freedoms, is section 251 justified by section 1 of the Canadian Charter of Rights

and Freedoms and therefore not inconsistent with the
Constitution Act, 1982?

Answer:

In respect of the violation of the right of a pregnant
woman to "security of the person" in s. 7 caused by s.
251 of the Criminal Code, s. 251 is not justified by s. 1
of the Charter.

3. **Question:**

Is section 251 of the Criminal Code of Canada *ultra
vires* the Parliament of Canada?

Answer:

No, in the sense that s. 251 is within the proper jurisdiction of Parliament on the basis of s. 91(27) of the
Constitution Act, 1867.

4. **Question:**

Does section 251 of the Criminal Code of Canada
violate section 96 of the Constitution Act, 1867?

Answer:

No.

5. **Question:**

Does section 251 of the Criminal Code of Canada
unlawfully delegate federal criminal power to
provincial Ministers of Health or Therapeutic Abortion Committees, and in doing so, has the Federal
Government abdicated its authority in this area?

Answer:

No.

6. **Question:**

Do sections 605 and 610(3) of the Criminal Code of
Canada infringe or deny the rights and freedoms
guaranteed by sections 7, 11(*d*), 11(*f*), 11(*h*) and
24(1) of the Canadian Charter of Rights and
Freedoms?

Answer:

With respect to s. 605, the answer is no. Whether or
not subs. 610(3) of the Criminal Code violates a

Charter right, I agree with the Court of Appeal that, whatever this Court's power to award costs in appeals such as this one, costs should not be awarded in this case.

7. **Question:**

If sections 605 and 610(3) of the Criminal Code of Canada infringe or deny the rights and freedoms guaranteed by sections 7, 11(*d*), 11(*f*1), 11(*h*) and 24(1) of the Canadian Charter of Rights and Freedoms, are sections 605 and 610(3) justified by section 1 of the Canadian Charter of Rights and Freedoms and therefore not inconsistent with the Constitution Act, 1982?

Answer:

Given the answer to question 6, this question does not call for an answer.

On the basis of my answers to the first two constitutional questions, I would allow the appeal.

Reasons for Judgment:
Justice Bertha Wilson

At the heart of this appeal is the question whether a pregnant woman can, as a constitutional matter, be compelled by law to carry the foetus to term. The legislature has proceeded on the basis that she can be so compelled and, indeed, has made it a criminal offence punishable by imprisonment under s. 251 of the Criminal Code, R.S.C. 1970, c. C-34, for her or her physician to terminate the pregnancy unless the procedural requirements of the section are complied with.

My colleagues, the Chief Justice and Beetz J., have attacked those requirements in reasons which I have had the privilege of reading. They have found that the requirements do not comport with the principles of fundamental justice in the procedural sense and have concluded that, since they cannot be severed from the provisions creating the substantive offence, the whole of s. 251 must fall.

With all due respect, I think that the Court must tackle the primary issue first. A consideration as to whether or not the procedural requirements for obtaining or performing an abortion comport with fundamental justice is purely academic if such requirements cannot as a constitutional matter be imposed at all. If a pregnant woman cannot, as a constitutional matter, be compelled by law to carry the foetus to term against her will, a review of the procedural requirements by which she may be compelled to do so seems pointless. Moreover, it would, in my opinion, be an exercise in futility for the legislature to expend its time and energy in attempting to remedy the defects in the procedural requirements unless it has some assurance that this process will, at the end of the day, result in the creation of a valid criminal offence. I turn, therefore, to what I believe is the central issue that must be addressed.

1. The Right of Access to Abortion

Section 7 of the Charter provides:

> 7. Everyone has the right to life, liberty and security of the person and the right not to be deprived thereof except in accordance with the principles of fundamental justice.

I agree with the Chief Justice that we are not called upon in this case to delineate the full content of the right to life, liberty and security of the person. This would be an impossible task because we cannot envisage all the contexts in which such a right might be asserted. What we are asked to do, I believe, is define the content of the right in the context of the legislation under attack. Does s. 251 of the Criminal Code which limits the pregnant woman's access to abortion violate her right to life, liberty and security of the person within the meaning of s. 7?

Leaving aside for the moment the implications of the section for the foetus and addressing only the s. 7 right of the pregnant woman, it seems to me that we can say with a fair degree of confidence that a legislative scheme for the obtaining of an abortion which exposes the pregnant woman to a threat would violate her right under s. 7. Indeed, we have already stated in *Singh v. Minister of Employment and Immigration*, [1985] 1 S.C.R. 177, that security of the person even on the purely physical level must encompass freedom from the threat of physical punishment or suffering as well as freedom from the actual punishment or suffering itself. In other words, the fact of exposure is enough to violate security of the person. I agree with the Chief Justice and Beetz J. who, for differing reasons, find that pregnant women are exposed to a threat to their physical and psychological security under the legislative scheme set up in s. 251 and, since these are aspects of their security of the person, their s. 7 right is accordingly violated. But this, of course, does not answer the question whether even the ideal legislative scheme, assuming that it is one which poses no *threat* to the physical and psychological security of the person of the pregnant woman, would be valid under s. 7. I say this for two reasons: (1) because s. 7 encompasses more than the right to security of the person; it speaks also of the right to liberty, and (2) because security of the person may encompass more than physical and psychological security; this we have yet to decide.

It seems to me, therefore, that to commence the analysis with the premise that the s. 7 right encompasses only a right to physical and psychological security and to fail to deal with the right to liberty in the context of "life, liberty and security of the person" begs the central issue in the case. If either the right to liberty or the right to security of the person or a combination of both confers on the pregnant woman the right to decide for herself (with the guidance of her physician) whether or not to have an abortion, then we have to examine the legislative scheme not only from the point of view of fundamental justice in the procedural sense but in the substantive sense as well. I think, therefore, that we must answer the question: what is meant by the right to liberty in the context of the abortion issue? Does it, as Mr. Manning suggests, give the pregnant woman control over decisions affecting her own body? If not, does her right to security of the person give her such control? I turn first to the right of liberty.

(a) The Right to Liberty

In order to ascertain the content of the right to liberty we must, as Dickson C.J. stated in *R. v. Big M Drug Mart Ltd.*, [1985] 1 S.C.R. 295, commence with an analysis of the purpose of the right. Quoting from the Chief Justice at p. 344:

> . . . the purpose of the right or freedom in question is to be sought by reference to the character and the larger objects of the Charter itself, to the language chosen to articulate the specific right or freedom, to the historical origins of the concepts enshrined, and where applicable, to the meaning and purpose of the other specific rights and freedoms with which it is associated within the text of the Charter. The interpretation should be, as the judgment in *Southam* emphasizes, a generous rather than a legalistic one, aimed at fulfilling the purpose of the guarantee and securing for individuals the full benefit of the Charter's protection.

We are invited, therefore, to consider the purpose of the Charter in general and of the right to liberty in particular.

The Charter is predicated on a particular conception of the place of the individual in society. An individual is not a totally independent entity disconnected from the society in which he or she lives. Neither, however, is the individual a mere cog in an impersonal machine in which his or her values, goals and aspirations are subordinated to those of the collectivity. The individual is a bit of both. The Charter reflects this reality by leaving a wide range of activities and decisions open to legitimate government control while at the same time placing limits on the proper scope of that control. Thus, the rights guaranteed in the Charter erect around each individual, metaphorically speaking, an invisible fence over which the state will not be allowed to trespass. The role of the courts is to map out, piece by piece, the parameters of the fence.

The Charter and the right to individual liberty guaranteed under it are inextricably tied to the concept of human dignity. Professor Neil MacCormick,* *Legal Right and Social Democracy: Essays in Legal and Political Philosophy*, speaks of liberty as "a condition of human self-respect and of that contentment which resides in the ability to pursue one's own conception of a full and rewarding life" (p. 39). He says at p. 41:

> To be able to decide what to do and how to do it, to carry out one's own decisions and accept their consequences, seems to me essential to one's self-respect as a human being, and essential to the possibility of that contentment. Such self-respect and contentment are in my judgment fundamental goods for human beings, the worth of life itself being on condition of having or striving for them. If a person were deliberately denied the opportunity of self-respect and that contentment, he would suffer deprivation of his essential humanity.

Dickson C.J. in *R. v. Big M Drug Mart Ltd.* makes the same point at p. 346:

* Regius Professor of Public Law and the Law of Nature and Nations, University of Edinburgh.

It should also be noted, however, than an emphasis on individual conscience and individual judgment also lies at the heart of our democratic political tradition. The ability of each citizen to make free and informed decisions is the absolute prerequisite for the legitimacy, acceptability, and efficacy of our system of self-government. It is because of the centrality of the rights associated with freedom of individual conscience both to basic beliefs about human worth and dignity and to a free and democratic political system that American jurisprudence has emphasized the primacy or "firstness" of the First Amendment. It is this same centrality that in my view underlies their designation in the Canadian Charter of Rights and Freedoms as "fundamental". They are the *sine qua non* of the political tradition underlying the Charter.

It was further amplified in Dickson C.J.'s discussion of Charter interpretation in *R. v. Oakes*, [1986] 1 S.C.R. 103, at p. 136:

A second contextual element of interpretation of s. 1 is provided by the words "free and democratic society". Inclusion of these words as the final standard of justification for limits on rights and freedoms refers the Courts to the very purpose for which the Charter was originally entrenched in the Constitution: Canadian society is to be free and democratic. The Court must be guided by the values and principles essential to a free and democratic society which I believe embody, to name but a few, respect for the inherent dignity of the human person, commitment to social justice and equality, accommodation of a wide variety of beliefs, respect for cultural and group identity, and faith in social and political institutions which enhance the participation of individuals and groups in society. The underlying values and principles of a free and democratic society are the genesis of the rights and freedoms guaranteed by the Charter and the ultimate standard against which a limit on a right or freedom must be shown, despite its effect, to be reasonable and demonstrably justified.

The idea of human dignity finds expression in almost every right and freedom guaranteed in the Charter. Individuals are afforded the right to choose their own religion and their own philosophy of life, the right to choose with whom they will associate and how they will express themselves, the right to choose where they will live and what occupation they will pursue. These are all examples of the basic theory underlying the Charter, namely that the state will respect choices made by individuals and, to the greatest extent possible, will avoid subordinating these choices to any one conception of the good life.

Thus, an aspect of the respect for human dignity on which the Charter is found is the right to make fundamental personal decisons without interference from the state. This right is a critical component of the right to liberty. Liberty, as was noted in *Singh*, is a phrase capable of a broad range of meaning. In my view, this right, properly construed, grants the individual a degree of autonomy in making decisions of fundamental personal importance.

This view is consistent with the position I took in the case of *R. v. Jones*, [1986] 2 S.C.R. 284. One issue raised in that case was whether the right to liberty in s. 7 of the Charter included a parent's right to bring up his children in accordance with his conscientious beliefs. In concluding that it did I stated at pp. 318-19:

> I believe that the framers of the Constitution in guaranteeing "liberty" as a fundamental value in a free and democratic society had in mind the freedom of the individual to develop and realize his potential to the full, to plan his own life to suit his own character, to make his own choices for good or ill, to be nonconformist, idiosyncratic and even eccentric — to be, in today's parlance, "his own person" and accountable as such. John Stuart Mill described it as "pursuing our own good in our own way". This, he believed, we

should be free to do "so long as we do not attempt to deprive others of theirs or impede their efforts to obtain it". He added:

> Each is the proper guardian of his own health, whether bodily or mental and spiritual. Mankind are greater gainers by suffering each other to live as seems good to themselves than by compelling each to live as seems good to the rest.

Liberty in a free and democratic society does not require the state to approve the personal decisions made by its citizens; it does, however, require the state to respect them.

This conception of the proper ambit of the right to liberty under our Charter is consistent with the American jurisprudence on the subject. While care must undoubtedly be taken to avoid a mechanical application of concepts developed in different cultural and constitutional contexts, I would respectfully agree with the observation of my colleague, Estey J., in *Law Society of Upper Canada v. Skapinker*, [1984] 1 S.C.R. 357, at pp. 366-67:

> With the Constitution Act, 1982 comes a new dimension, a new yardstick of reconciliation between the individual and the community and their respective rights, a dimension which, like the balance of the Constitution, remains to be interpreted and applied by the Court.
>
> The courts in the United States have had almost two hundred years experience at this task and it is of more than passing interest to those concerned with these new developments in Canada to study the experience of the United States courts.

As early as the 1920's the American Supreme Court employed the Fifth and Fourteenth Amendments of the Bill of Rights to give parents a degree of choice in the education of their children. In *Meyer v. Nebraska*, 262 U.S. 390 (1923), the Court struck down a law prohibiting the teaching of any subject in a language other than English. In *Pierce v. Society of Sisters*, 268 U.S. 510 (1925), an Oregon statute requiring all "normal children" to attend public school and thus prohibiting private school attendance was held to be unconstitutional. The Court in *Pierce* at pp. 534-35 characterized the interest being infringed as "the liberty of parents and guardians to direct the upbringing and education of children under their control".

The sanctity of the family was underlined by the decision in *Skinner v. Oklahoma*, 316 U.S. 535 (1942), where the Supreme Court invalidated a state law authorizing the sterilization of individuals convicted of two or more crimes involving moral turpitude. While the law was struck down on the basis that it violated the equal protection clause of the Fourteenth Amendment, the Court had this to say of the interest at stake: "We are dealing here with legislation which involves one of the basic civil rights of man. Marriage and procreation are fundamental to the very existence and survival of the race" (at p. 541).

Later the Supreme Court was asked to determine the constitutionality of a Connecticut statute forbidding the use of contraceptives by married couples. In *Griswold v. Connecticut*, 381 U.S. 479 (1965), the majority held this statute to be invalid. The judges writing for the majority used various constitutional routes to arrive at this conclusion but the common denominator seems to have been a profound concern over the invasion of the marital home required for the enforcement of the law. *Griswold* was interpreted by the Supreme Court in the later case of *Eisenstadt v. Baird*, 405 U.S. 438 (1972), where the majority stated at p. 453:

It is true that in *Griswold* the right of privacy in question inhered in the marital relationship. Yet the marital couple is not an independent entity with a mind and heart of its own, but an association of two individuals each with a separate intellectual and emotional make up. If the right of privacy means anything, it is the right of the *individual*, married or single, to be free from unwarranted governmental intrusion into matters so fundamentally affecting a person as the decision whether to bear or beget a child.

In *Eisenstadt* the Court struck down a Massachusetts law that prohibited the distribution of any drug for the purposes of contraception to unmarried persons on the ground that it violated the equal protection clause.

The equal protection clause was also used by the Supreme Court in *Loving v. Virginia*, 388 U.S. 1 (1967), to strike down legislation that purported to forbid inter-racial marriage. The Court tied its decision to the previous line of cases that protected basic choices relating to family life. It stated at p. 12: "The freedom to marry has long been recognized as one of the 'vital' personal rights essential to the orderly pursuit of happiness by free men. Marriage is one of the 'basic civil rights of man', fundamental to our very existence and survival . . . [The] freedom to marry . . . resides with the individual . . ." Thus, by a process of accretion the scope of the right of individuals to make fundamental decisions affecting their private lives was elaborated in the United States on a case by case basis. The parameters of the fence were being progressively defined.

For our purposes the most interesting development in this area of American law are the decisions of the Supreme Court in *Roe v. Wade*, 410 U.S. 113 (1973), and its sister case *Doe v. Bolton*, 410 U.S. 179 (1973). In *Roe v. Wade* the Court held that a pregnant woman has the right to decide whether or not to terminate her pregnancy. This conclusion, the majority stated, was mandated by the body of existing law ensuring that the state would not be allowed to interfere with certain fundamental personal decisions such as education, child-rearing, procreation, marriage and contraception. The Court concluded that the right to privacy found in the Fourteenth Amendment guarantee of liberty " . . . is broad enough to encompass a woman's decision whether or not to terminate her pregnancy" (p. 153).

This right was not, however, to be taken as absolute. At some point the legitimate state interests in the protection of health, proper medical standards, and pre-natal life would justify its qualifications. Professor Tribe,* *American Constitutional Law* (1978), conveniently summarizes the limits the Court found to be inherent in the woman's right. I quote from pp. 924-25:

> Specifically, the Court held that, because the woman's right to decide whether or not to end a pregnancy is fundamental, only a compelling interest can justify state regulation impinging in any way upon that right. During the first trimester of pregnancy, when abortion is less hazardous in terms of the woman's life than carrying the child to term would be, the state may require only that the abortion be performed by a licensed physician; no further regulations peculiar to abortion as such are compellingly justified in that period.
>
> After the first trimester, the compelling state interest in the mother's health permits it to adopt reasonable regulations in order to promote safe abortions — but requiring abortions to be performed in hospitals, or only after approval of another doctor or committee in addition to the woman's physician, is impermissible, as is requiring that the abortion procedure employ a technique that, however preferable from a medical perspective, is not widely available.
>
> Once the fetus is viable, in the sense that it is capable of survival outside the uterus with artificial aid, the state interest in preserving the fetus becomes compelling, and the state may thus proscribe its premature

* Professor of Law, Harvard University.

removal (i.e., its abortion) except to preserve the mother's life or health.

The decision in *Roe v. Wade* was re-affirmed by the Supreme Court in *City of Akron v. Akron Centre for Reproductive Health Inc.*, 462 U.S. 416 (1983), and again, though by a bare majority, in *Thornburgh v. American College of Obstetricians and Gynecologists*, 106 S. Ct. 2169 (1986). In *Thornburgh*, Blackmun J., speaking for the majority, identifies the core value which the American courts have found to inhere in the concept of liberty. He states at pp. 2184-85:

> Our cases long have recognized that the Constitution embodies a promise that a certain private sphere of individual liberty will be kept largely beyond the reach of government . . . [citations omitted] That promise extends to women as well as to men. Few decisions are more personal and intimate, more properly private, or more basic to individual dignity and autonomy, than a woman's decision — with the guidance of her physician and within the limits specified in *Roe* — whether to end her pregnancy. A woman's right to make that choice freely is fundamental. Any other result, in our view, would protect inadequately a central part of the sphere of liberty that our law guarantees equally to all.

In my opinion, the respect for individual decision-making in matters of fundamental personal importance reflected in the American jurisprudence also informs the Canadian Charter. Indeed, as the Chief Justice pointed out in *R. v. Big M Drug Mart Ltd.*, beliefs about human worth and dignity "are the *sine qua non* of the political tradition underlying the Charter". I would conclude, therefore, that the right to liberty contained in s. 7 guarantees to every individual a degree of personal autonomy over important decisions intimately affecting their private lives.

The question then becomes whether the decision of a

woman to terminate her pregnancy falls within this class of protected decisions. I have no doubt that it does. This decision is one that will have profound psychological, economic and social consequences for the pregnant woman. The circumstances giving rise to it can be complex and varied and there may be, and usually are, powerful considerations militating in opposite directions. It is a decision that deeply reflects the way the woman thinks about herself and her relationship to others and to society at large. It is not just a medical decision; it is a profound social and ethical one as well. Her response to it will be the response of the whole person.

It is probably impossible for a man to respond, even imaginatively, to such a dilemma not just because it is outside the realm of his personal experience (although this is, of course, the case) but because he can relate to it only by objectifying it, thereby eliminating the subjective elements of the female psyche which are at the heart of the dilemma. As Noreen Burrows* has pointed out in her essay on "International Law and Human Rights: the Case of Women's Rights", in *Human Rights: From Rhetoric to Reality*, the history of the struggle for human rights from the eighteenth century on has been the history of men struggling to assert their dignity and common humanity against an overbearing state apparatus. The more recent struggle for women's rights has been a struggle to eliminate discrimination, to achieve a place for women in a man's world, to develop a set of legislative reforms in order to place women in the same position as men (pp. 81-82). It has not been a struggle to define the rights of women in relation to their special place in the societal structure and in relation to the biological distinction between the two sexes. Thus, women's needs and aspirations are only now being translated into protected rights. The right to reproduce

* Lecturer in European Law, University of Glasgow.

or not to reproduce which is in issue in this case is one such right and is properly perceived as an integral part of modern woman's struggle to assert her dignity and worth as a human being.

Given then that the right to liberty guaranteed by s. 7 of the Charter gives a woman the right to decide for herself whether or not to terminate her pregnancy, does s. 251 of the Criminal Code violate this right? Clearly it does. The purpose of the section is to take the decision away from the woman and give it to a committee. Furthermore, as the Chief Justice correctly points out, the committee bases its decision on "criteria entirely unrelated to [the pregnant woman's] priorities and aspirations". The fact that the decision whether a woman will be allowed to terminate her pregnancy is in the hands of a committee is just as great a violation of the woman's right to personal autonomy in decisions of an intimate and private nature as it would be if a committee were established to decide whether a woman should be allowed to continue her pregnancy. Both these arrangements violate the woman's right to liberty by deciding for her something that she has the right to decide for herself.

(b) The Right to Security of Person

Section 7 of the Charter also guarantees everyone the right to security of the person. Does this, as Mr. Manning suggests, extend to the right of control over their own bodies?

I agree with the Chief Justice and with Beetz J. that the right to "security of the person" under s. 7 of the Charter protects both the physical and psychological integrity of the individual. State enforced medical or surgical treatment comes readily to mind as an obvious invasion of physical integrity. Lamer J. held in *Mills v. The Queen*, [1986] 1 S.C.R. 863, that the right to security of the person entitled a person to be protected against psychological trauma as well — in that case the psychological trauma resulting from delays in the trial process under s. 11(*b*) of the Charter. He found that psychological trauma could take the form of "stigmatization of the accused, loss of privacy, stress and anxiety resulting from a multitude of factors, including possible disruption of family, social life and work, legal costs and uncertainty as to outcome and sanction". I agree with my colleague and I think that his comments are very germane to the instant case because, as the Chief Justice and Beetz J. point out, the present legislative scheme for the obtaining of an abortion clearly subjects pregnant women to considerable emotional stress as well as to unnecessary physical risk. I believe, however, that the flaw in the present legislative scheme goes much deeper than that. In essence, what it does is assert that the woman's capacity to reproduce is not to be subject to her own control. It is to be subject to the control of the state. She may not choose whether to exercise her existing capacity or not to exercise it. This is not, in my view, just a matter of interfering with her right to liberty in the sense (already discussed) of her right to personal autonomy in decision-making, it is a direct interference with her physical "person" as well. She is truly being treated as a means — a means to an end which she does not desire but over which she has no control. She is the passive recipient of a decision made by others as to whether her body is to be used to nurture a new life. Can there be anything that comports less with human dignity and self-respect? How can a woman in this position have any sense of security with respect to her person? I believe that s. 251 of the Criminal Code deprives the pregnant woman of her right to security of the person as well as her right to liberty.

2. *The Scope of the Right under s. 7*

I turn now to a consideration of the degree of personal autonomy the pregnant woman has under s. 7 of the Charter when faced with a decision whether or not to have an abortion or, to put it into the legislative context, the degree to which the legislature can deny the pregnant woman access to abortion without violating her s. 7 right. This involves a consideration of the extent to which the legislature can "deprive" her of it under the second part of s. 7 and the extent to which it can put "limits" on it under s. 1.

(a) The Principles of Fundamental Justice

Does s. 251 deprive women of their right to liberty and to security of the person "in accordance with the principles of fundamental justice"? I agree with Lamer J. who stated in *Re B.C. Motor Vehicle Act*, [1985] 2 S.C.R. 486, at p. 513, that the principles of fundamental justice "cannot be given any exhaustive content or simple enumerative definition, but will take on concrete meaning as the courts address alleged violations of s. 7". In the same judgment Lamer J. also stated at p. 503:

> In other words, the principles of fundamental justice are to be found in the basic tenets of our legal system. They do not lie in the realm of general public policy but in the inherent domain of the judiciary as guardian of the justice system. Such an approach to the interpretation of "principles of fundamental justice" is consistent with the wording and structure of s. 7, the context of the section, *i.e.*, ss. 8 to 14, and the character and larger objects of the Charter itself. It provides meaningful content for the s. 7 guarantee all the while avoiding adjudication of policy matters.

While Lamer J. draws mainly upon ss. 8 to 14 of the Charter to give substantive content to the principles of fundamental justice, he does not preclude, but seems rather to encourage, the idea that recourse may be had to other rights guaranteed by the Charter for the same purpose. The question, therefore, is whether the deprivation of the s. 7 right is in accordance not only with procedural fairness (and I agree with the Chief Justice and Beetz J. for the reasons they give that it is not) but also with the fundamental rights and freedoms laid down elsewhere in the Charter.

This approach to s. 7 is supported by comments made by La Forest J. in *Lyons v. The Queen*, [1987] 2 S.C.R. 309. He urged that the rights enshrined in the Charter should not be read in isolation. Rather, he states:

> . . . the Charter protects a complex of interacting values, each more or less fundamental to the free and democratic society that is Canada (*R. v. Oakes*, [1986] 1 S.C.R. 103, at 136), and the particularization of rights and freedoms contained in the Charter thus represents a somewhat artificial, if necessary and intrinsically worthwhile attempt to structure and focus the judicial exposition of such rights and freedoms. The necessity of structuring the discussion should not, however, lead us to overlook the importance of appreciating the manner in which the amplifications of the content of each enunciated right and freedom imbues and informs our understandings of the value structure sought to be protected by the Charter as a whole and, in particular, of the content of the other specific rights and freedoms it embodies.

I believe, therefore, that a deprivation of the s. 7 right which has the effect of infringing a right guaranteed elsewhere in the Charter cannot be in accordance with the principles of fundamental justice.

In my view, the deprivation of the s. 7 right with which we are concerned in this case offends s. 2(*a*) of the Charter. I say this because I believe that the decision whether or not to terminate a pregnancy is essentially a moral decision, a matter of conscience. I do not think there is or can be any dispute about that. The question is: whose conscience? I believe, for the reasons I gave in discussing the right to liberty, that in a free and democratic society it must be the conscience of the individual. Indeed, s. 2(*a*) makes it clear that this freedom belongs to "everyone", *i.e.*, to each of us individually. I quote the section for convenience:

> 2. Everyone has the following fundamental freedoms:
>   (a) freedom of conscience and religion;

In *R. v. Big M Drug Mart Ltd.*, *supra*, Dickson C.J. made some very insightful comments about the nature of the right enshrined in s. 2(*a*) of the Charter at pp. 345-47:

> Beginning, however, with the Independent faction within the Parliamentary party during the Commonwealth or Interregnum, many, even those who shared the basic beliefs of the ascendent religion, came to voice opposition to the use of the State's coercive power to secure obedience to religious precepts and to extirpate non-conforming beliefs. The basis of this opposition was no longer simply a conviction that the State was enforcing the wrong set of beliefs and practices but rather the perception that belief itself was not amenable to compulsion. Attempts to compel belief or practice denied the reality of individual conscience and dishonoured the God that had planted it in His creatures. It is from these antecedents that the concepts of freedom of religion and freedom of conscience became associated, to form, as they do in s. 2(*a*) of our Charter, the single integrated concept of "freedom of conscience and religion".
>
> What unites enunciated freedoms in the American First Amendment, in s. 2(*a*) of the Charter and in the provisions of other human rights documents in which they are associated *is the notion of the centrality of individual conscience and the inappropriateness of governmental intervention to compel or to constrain*

its manifestation. In *Hunter v. Southam Inc.*, *supra*, the purpose of the Charter was identified, at p. 155, as "the unremitting protection of individual rights and liberties". It is easy to see the relationship between respect for individual conscience and the valuation of human dignity that motivates such unremitting protection.

It should also be noted, however, that an emphasis on individual conscience and individual judgment also lies at the heart of our democratic political tradition. *The ability of each citizen to make free and informed decisions is the absolute prerequisite for the legitimacy, acceptability, and efficacy of our system of self-government.* It is because of the centrality of the rights associated with freedom of individual conscience both to basic beliefs about human worth and dignity and to a free and democratic political system that American jurisprudence has emphasized the primacy or "firstness" of the First Amendment. It is this same centrality that in my view underlies their designation in the Canadian Charter of Rights and Freedoms as "fundamental". They are the *sine qua non* of the political tradition underlying the Charter.

Viewed in this context, the purpose of freedom of conscience and religion becomes clear. *The values that underlie our political and philosophic traditions demand that every individual be free to hold and to manifest whatever beliefs and opinions his or her conscience dictates, provided* inter alia *only that such manifestations do not injure his or her neighbours or their parallel rights to hold and manifest beliefs and opinions of their own*. Religious belief and practice are historically prototypical and, in many ways, paradigmatic of conscientiously-held beliefs and manifestations and are therefore protected by the Charter. Equally protected, and for the same reasons, are expressions and manifestations of religious non-belief and refusals to participate in religious practice. It may perhaps be that freedom of conscience and religion extends beyond these principles to prohibit other sorts of governmental involvement in matters having to do with religion. For the present case it is sufficient in my opinion to say that whatever else freedom of conscience and religion may mean, it must at the very least mean this: government may not coerce individuals to affirm a specific religious belief or to manifest a specific religious practice for a sectarian purpose. I leave to another case the degree, if any, to which the government may, to achieve a vital interest or objective, engage in coercive action which s. 2(*a*) might otherwise prohibit. [My emphasis.]

The Chief Justice sees religious belief and practice as the paradigmatic example of conscientiously-held beliefs and manifestations and as such protected by the Charter. But I do not think he is saying that a personal morality which is not founded in religion is outside the protection of s. 2(*a*). Certainly, it would be my view that conscientious beliefs which are not religiously motivated are equally protected by freedom of conscience in s. 2(*a*). In so saying I am not unmindful of the fact that the Charter opens with an affirmation that "Canada is founded upon principles that recognize the supremacy of God..." But I am also mindful that the values entrenched in the Charter are those which characterize a free and democratic society.

As is pointed out by Professor C.E.M. Joad*: *Guide to the Philosophy of Morals and Politics*, the role of the state in a democracy is to establish the background conditions under which individual citizens may pursue the ethical values which in their view underlie the good life. He states at p. 801:

> For the welfare of the state is nothing apart from the good of the citzens who compose it. It is no doubt true that a State whose citizens are compelled to go right is more efficient than one whose citizens are free to go wrong. But what then? To sacrifice freedom in the interests of efficiency, is to sacrifice what confers upon

* Then Head of Department of Philosophy and Psychology, Birkbeck College, University of London.

human beings their humanity. It is no doubt easy to govern a flock of sheep; but there is no credit in the governing, and, if the sheep were born as men, no virtue in the sheep.

Professor Joad further emphasizes at p. 803 that individuals in a democratic society can never be treated "merely as means to ends beyond themselves" because:

To the right of the individual to be treated as an end, which entails his right to the full development and expression of his personality, all other rights and claims must, the democrat holds, be subordinated. I do not know how this principle is to be defended any more than I can frame a defence for the principles of democracy and liberty.

Professor Joad stresses that the essence of a democracy is its recognition of the fact that the state is made for man and not man for the state (p. 805). He firmly rejects the notion that science provides a basis for subordinating the individual to the state. He says at pp. 805-06:

Human beings, it is said, are important only in so far as they fit into a biological scheme or assist in the furtherance of the evolutionary process. Thus each generation of women must accept as its sole function the production of children who will constitute the next generation who, in their turn, will devote their lives and sacrifice their inclinations to the task of producing a further generation, and so on ad infinitum. This is the doctrine of eternal sacrifice — "jam yesterday, jam tomorrow, but never jam today". For, it may be asked, to what end should generations be produced, unless the individuals who compose them are valued in and for themselves, are, in fact, ends in themselves? There is no escape from the doctrine of the perpetual recurrence of generations who have value only in so far as they produce more generations, the perpetual subordination of citizens who have value only in so far as they promote the interests of the State to which they are subordinated, except in the individualist doctrine, which is also the Christian doctrine, that the individual is an end in himself.

It seems to me, therefore, that in a free and democratic society "freedom of conscience and religion" should be broadly construed to extend to conscientiously-held beliefs, whether grounded in religion or in a secular morality. Indeed, as a matter of statutory interpretation, "conscience" and "religion" should not be treated as tautologous if capable of independent, although related, meaning. Accordingly, for the state to take sides on the issue of abortion, as it does in the impugned legislation by making it a criminal offence for the pregnant woman to exercise one of her options, is not only to endorse but also to enforce, on pain of a further loss of liberty through actual imprisonment, one conscientiously-held view at the expense of another. It is to deny freedom of conscience to some, to treat them as means to an end, to deprive them, as Professor MacCormick puts it, of their "essential humanity". Can this comport with fundamental justice? Was Blackmun J. not correct when he said in *Thornburgh*, *supra*, at p. 2185:

A woman's right to make that choice freely is fundamental. Any other result . . . would protect inadequately a central part of the sphere of liberty that our law guarantees equally to all.

Legislation which violates freedom of conscience in this manner cannot, in my view, be in accordance with the principles of fundamental justice within the meaning of s. 7.

(b) Section 1 of the Charter

The majority of this Court held in *Re B.C. Motor Vehicle Act*, *supra*, that a deprivation of the s. 7 right in violation of the principles of fundamental justice in the substantive sense could nevertheless constitute a reasonable limit under s. 1 and be justified in a free and democratic society. It is necessary therefore to consider whether s. 251 of the Criminal Code can be saved under s. 1. The section provides:

> 1. The Canadian Charter of Rights and Freedoms guarantees the rights and freedoms set out in it subject only to such reasonable limits prescribed by law as can be demonstrably justified in a free and democratic society.

This section received judicial scrutiny by this Court in *R. v. Oakes*, *supra*. Dickson C.J., speaking for the majority, set out two criteria which must be met if the limit is to be found reasonable: (1) the objective which the legislation is designed to achieve must relate to concerns which are pressing and substantial; and (2) the means chosen must be proportional to the objective sought to be achieved. The Chief Justice identified three important components of proportionality at p. 139:

> First, the measures adopted must be carefully designed to achieve the objective in question. They must not be arbitrary, unfair or based on irrational considerations. In short, they must be rationally connected to the objective. Second, the means, even if rationally connected to the objective in the first sense, should impair "as little as possible" the right or freedom in question: *R. v. Big M Drug Mart Ltd.*, *supra*, at p. 352. Third, there must be a proportionality between the *effects* of the measures which are responsible for limiting the Charter right or freedom, and the objective which has been identified as of "sufficient importance".

Does s. 251 meet this test?

In my view, the primary objective of the impugned legislation must be seen as the protection of the foetus. It undoubtedly has other ancillary objectives, such as the protection of the life and health of pregnant women, but I believe that the main objective advanced to justify a restriction on the pregnant woman's s. 7 right is the protection of the foetus. I think this is a perfectly valid legislative objective.

Miss Wein submitted on behalf of the Crown that the Court of Appeal was correct in concluding that "the situation respecting a woman's right to control her own person becomes more complex when she becomes pregnant, and that some statutory control may be appropriate". I agree. I think s. 1 of the Charter authorizes reasonable limits to be put upon the woman's right having regard to the fact of the developing foetus within her body. The question is: at what point in the pregnancy does the protection of the foetus become such a pressing and substantial concern as to outweigh the fundamental right of the woman to decide whether or not to carry the foetus to term? At what point does the state's interest in the protection of the foetus become "compelling" and justify state intervention in what is otherwise a matter of purely personal and private concern?

In *Roe v. Wade*, *supra*, the United States Supreme Court held that the state's interest became compelling when the foetus became viable, *i.e.* when it could exist outside the body of the mother. As Miss Wein pointed out, no particular justification was advanced by the Court for the selection of viability as the relevant criterion. The Court expressly avoided the question as to when human life begins. Blackmun J. stated at p. 159:

> We need not resolve the difficult question of when life begins. When those trained in the respective disciplines of medicine, philosophy, and theology are unable to arrive at any consensus, the judiciary, at this point in the development of man's knowledge, is not in a position to speculate as to the answer.

He referred, therefore, to the developing foetus as "potential life" and to the state's interest as "the protection of potential life".

Miss Wein submitted that it was likewise not necessary for the Court in this case to decide when human life begins although she acknowledged that the value to be placed on "potential life" was significant in assessing the importance of the legislative objective sought to be achieved by s. 251. It would be my view, and I think it is consistent with the position taken by the United States Supreme Court in *Roe v. Wade*, that the value to be placed on the foetus as potential life is directly related to the stage of its development during gestation. The undeveloped foetus starts out as a newly fertilized ovum; the fully developed foetus emerges ultimately as an infant. A developmental progression takes place in between these two extremes and, in my opinion, this progression has a direct bearing on the value of the foetus as potential life. It is a fact of human experience that a miscarriage or spontaneous abortion of the foetus at six months is attended by far greater sorrow and sense of loss than a miscarriage or spontaneous abortion at six days or even six weeks. This is not, of course, to deny that the foetus is potential life from the moment of conception. Indeed, I agree with the observation of O'Connor J. dissenting in *City of Akron v. Akron Center for Reproductive Health, Inc.*, *supra*, at p. 461, (referred to by my colleague Beetz J. in his reasons) that the foetus is potential life from the moment of conception. It is simply to say that in balancing the state's interest in the protection of the foetus as potential life under s. 1 of the Charter against the right of the pregnant woman under s. 7 greater weight should be given to the state's interest in the later stages of pregnancy than in the earlier. The foetus should accordingly, for purposes of s. 1, be viewed in differential and developmental terms: see

Sumner*: *Abortion and Moral Theory*, pp. 125-28.

As Professor Sumner points out, both traditional approaches to abortion, the so-called "liberal" and "conservative" approaches, fail to take account of the essentially developmental nature of the gestation process. A developmental view of the foetus, on the other hand, supports a permissive approach to abortion in the early stages of pregnancy and a restrictive approach in the later stages. In the early stages the woman's autonomy would be absolute; her decision, reached in consultation with her physician, not to carry the foetus to term would be conclusive. The state would have no business inquiring into her reasons. Her reasons for having an abortion would, however, be the proper subject of inquiry at the later stages of her pregnancy when the state's compelling interest in the protection of the foetus would justify it in prescribing conditions. The precise point in the development of the foetus at which the state's interest in its protection becomes "compelling" I leave to the informed judgment of the legislature which is in a position to receive guidance on the subject from all the relevant disciplines. It seems to me, however, that it might fall somewhere in the second trimester. Indeed, according to Professor Sumner (p. 159), a differential abortion policy with a time limit in the second trimester is already in operation in the United States, Great Britain, France, Italy, Sweden, the Soviet Union, China, India, Japan and most of the countries of Eastern Europe although the time limits vary in these countries from the beginning to the end of the second trimester (*cf.* Isaacs, Stephen L., "Reproductive Rights 1983: An International Survey" (1982-83), 14 *Columbia Human Rights Law Review* 311, with respect to France and Italy).

Section 251 of the Criminal Code takes the decision

* Professor of Philosophy, University of Toronto.

away from the woman at all stages of her pregnancy. It is a complete denial of the woman's constitutionally protected right under s. 7, not merely a limitation on it. It cannot, in my opinion, meet the proportionality test in *Oakes*. It is not sufficiently tailored to the legislative objective and does not impair the woman's right "as little as possible". It cannot be saved under s. 1. Accordingly, even if the section were to be amended to remedy the purely procedural defects in the legislative scheme referred to by the Chief Justice and Beetz J. it would, in my opinion, still not be constitutionally valid.

One final word. I wish to emphasize that in these reasons I have dealt with the existence of the developing foetus merely as a factor to be considered in assessing the importance of the legislative objective under s. 1 of the Charter. I have not dealt with the entirely separate question whether a foetus is covered by the word "everyone" in s. 7 so as to have an independent right to life under that section. The Crown did not argue it and it is not necessary to decide it in order to dispose of the issues on this appeal.

3. Disposition

I would allow the appeal. I would strike down s. 251 of the Criminal Code as having no force and effect under s. 52(1) of the Constitution Act, 1982. I would answer the first constitutional question in the affirmative as regards s. 7 of the Charter and the second constitutional question in the negative. I would answer questions 3, 4 and 5 in the negative and question 6 in the manner proposed by Beetz J. It is not necessary to answer question 7.

I endorse the Chief Justice's critical comments on Mr. Manning's concluding remarks to the jury.

Dissenting Reasons:
Justice William McIntyre

Concurred in by
Justice Gerard La Forest

I have read the reasons for judgment prepared by my colleagues, the Chief Justice and Beetz and Wilson JJ. I agree that the principal issue which arises is whether s. 251 of the Criminal Code, R.S.C. 1970, c. C-34, contravenes s. 7 of the Canadian Charter of Rights and Freedoms. I will make some comments later on other issues put forward by the appellants. The Chief Justice has set out the constitutional questions and the relevant statutory provisions, as well as the facts and procedural history. He has considered the scope of s. 7 of the Charter and, having found that it has been offended, he would allow the appeal. I am unable to agree with his reasons or his disposition of the appeal. I find myself in broad general agreement with the reasons of the Court of Appeal, and I would dismiss the appeal on that basis and for reasons that I will endeavour to set forth.

Section 251 of the Criminal Code

I would say at the outset that it may be thought that this case does not raise the Charter issues which were argued and which have been addressed in the reasons of my colleagues. The charge here is one of conspiracy to breach the provisions of s. 251 of the Criminal Code. There is no doubt, and it has never been questioned, that the appellants adopted a course which was clearly in defiance of the provisions of the Code and it is difficult to see where any infringement of their rights, under s. 7 of the Charter, could have occurred. There is no female person involved in the case who has been denied a therapeutic abortion and, as a result, the whole argument on the right to security of the person, under s. 7 of the Charter, has been on a hypothetical basis. The case, however, was addressed by all the parties on that basis and the Court has accepted that position.

Sections 251(1) and (2) of the Criminal Code make it an indictable offence for a person to use any means to procure the miscarriage of a female person and prescribe on conviction a maximum sentence of two years' imprisonment, in the case of the woman herself, and a maximum sentence of life imprisonment in the case of another person. Parliament has decreed that procuring a non-therapeutic abortion is a crime deserving of severe punishment. Subsection (4) provides that subss. (1) and (2) shall not apply where an abortion is performed in accordance with subss. (4)(*a*), (*b*), (*c*) and (*d*). These subsections provide that a qualified medical practitioner may perform an abortion, and a pregnant woman may permit an abortion, in an accredited or an approved hospital where the therapeutic abortion committee for the hospital (defined in subs. (6)) has given its certificate in writing, stating that in its opinion the continuation of the woman's pregnancy would or would be likely to endanger her life or health. The certificate may be given to a qualified medical practitioner only after the committee, by a majority of its members and at a meeting where the woman's case has been reviewed, has authorized the giving of the certificate. Subsection (5) empowers the Minister of Health of a province to require a therapeutic abortion committee to furnish copies of certificates issued by the committee and such other information relating to the issuing of the certificate as he may require, and gives the Minister power to require similar information from a medical practitioner who has procured an abortion. Subsection (6) is the definitional section. It is clear from the foregoing that abortion is prohibited and that subs. (4) provides relieving provisions allowing an abortion in certain limited circumstances. It cannot be said that s. 251 of the Criminal Code confers any general right to have or to procure an abortion. On the contrary, the provision is aimed at protecting the interests of the unborn child and only lifts the criminal sanction where an abortion is necessary to protect the life or health of the mother.

In considering the constitutionality of s. 251 of the Criminal Code, it is first necessary to understand the background of this litigation and some of the problems which it raises. Section 251 of the Code has been denounced as ill-conceived and inadequate by those at one extreme of the abortion debate and as immoral and unacceptable by those at the opposite extreme. There are those, like the appellants, who assert that on moral and ethical grounds there is a simple solution to the problem: the inherent "right of women to control their own bodies" requires the repeal of s. 251 in favour of the principle of "abortion on demand". Opposing this view are those who contend with equal vigour, and also on moral and ethical grounds, for a clear and simple solution: the inherent "right to life of the unborn child" requires the repeal of s. 251(4), (5), (6) and (7) in order to leave an absolute ban on abortions. The battle lines so drawn are firmly held and the attitudes of the opposing parties admit of no compromise. From the submission of the Attorney General of Canada (set out in his factum at para. 6), however, it may appear that a majority in Canada do not see the issue in such black and white terms. Paragraph 6 is in these words:

> The evidence of opinion surveys indicates that there is a surprising consistency over the years and in different survey groups in the spectrum of opinions on the issue of abortion. Roughly 21 to 23% of people at one end of the spectrum are of the view, on the one hand, that abortion is a matter solely for the decision of the pregnant woman and that any legislation on this subject is unwarranted interference with a woman's right to deal with her own body, while about 19 to 20% are of the view, on the other hand, that destruction of the living fetus is the killing of human life and tantamount to murder. The remainder of the population (about 60%) are of the view that abortion should be prohibited in some circumstances.

Parliament has heeded neither extreme. Instead, an attempt has been made to balance the competing interests of the unborn child and the pregnant woman. Where the provisions of s. 251(4) are met, the abortion may be performed without legal sanction. Where they are not, abortion is deemed to be socially undesirable and is punished as a crime. In *Morgentaler v. The Queen*, [1976] 1 S.C.R. 616 [hereinafter *Morgentaler (1975)*], Laskin C.J. said (in dissent, but not on this point), at p. 627:

> What is patent on the face of the prohibitory portion of s. 251 is that Parliament has in its judgment decreed that interference by another, or even by the pregnant woman herself with the ordinary course of conception is socially undesirable conduct subject to punishment. That was a judgment open to Parliament in the exercise of its plenary criminal law power, and the fact that there

may be safe ways of terminating a pregnancy or that any woman or women claim a personal privilege to that end, becomes immaterial. I need cite no authority for the proposition that Parliament may determine what is not criminal as well as what is, and may hence introduce dispensations or exemptions in its criminal legislation.

Parliament's view that abortion is, in its nature, "socially undesirable conduct" is not new. Parliament's policy, as expressed by s. 251 of the Code, is consistent with that which has governed Canadian criminal law since Confederation and before: see Dickson J. (as he then was) in *Morgentaler (1975)*, *supra*, at p. 672, and the reasons of the Ontario Court of Appeal in this case: 52 O.R. (2d) 353, at pp. 364-66. It is against this background that I turn to the question of judicial review in light of the Charter.

Scope of Judicial Review under the Charter

Before the adoption of the Charter, there was little question of the limits of judicial review of the criminal law. For all practical purposes it was limited to a determination of whether the impugned enactment dealt with a subject which could fall within the criminal law power in s. 91(27) of the Constitution Act, 1867. There was no doubt of the power of Parliament to say what was and what was not criminal and to prohibit criminal conduct with penal sanctions, although from 1960 onwards legislation was subject to review under the Canadian Bill of Rights: see *Morgentaler*, *supra*. The adoption of the Charter brought a significant change. The power of judicial review of legislation acquired greater scope but, in my view, that scope is not unlimited and should be carefully confined to that which is ordained by the Charter. I am well aware that there will be disagreement about what was ordained by the Charter and, of course, a measure of interpretation of the Charter will be required in order to give substance and reality to its provisions. But the courts must not, in the guise of interpretation, postulate rights and freedoms which do not have a firm and a reasonably identifiable base in the Charter. In his reasons, the Chief Justice refers to the problem. He says:

> During argument before this Court, counsel for the Crown emphasized repeatedly that it is not the role of the judiciary in Canada to evaluate the wisdom of legislation enacted by our democratically elected representatives, or to second-guess difficult policy choices that confront all governments. In *Morgentaler v. The Queen*, [1976] 1 S.C.R. 616 at p. 671, I stressed that the Court had "not been called upon to decide, or even to enter, the loud and continuous public debate on abortion". Eleven years later, the controversy persists, and it remains true that this Court cannot presume to resolve all of the competing claims advanced in vigorous and healthy public debate. Courts and legislators in other democratic societies have reached completely contradictory decisions when asked to weigh the competing values relevant to the abortion question. See, *e.g. Roe v. Wade*, 410 U.S. 113 (1973), (United States Supreme Court); *Paton v. United Kingdom* (1980), 3 E.H.R.R. (European Court of Human Rights); *The Abortion Decision of the Federal Constitutional Court - First Senate - of the Federal Republic of Germany*, February 25, 1975, translated and reprinted in (1976), 9 John Marshall J. Prac. and Proc. 605; and the Abortion Act 1967, 1967 c. 87 (U.K.).
>
> But since 1976, and the first *Morgentaler* decision, the Court has been given added responsibilities. I stated in *Morgentaler (1975)*, at p. 671, that
>
> > the values we must accept for the purposes of this appeal are those expressed by Parliament which holds the view that the desire of a woman to be

relieved of her pregnancy is not, of itself, justification for performing an abortion.

Although no doubt it is still fair to say that courts are not the appropriate forum for articulating complex and controversial programmes of public policy, Canadian courts are now charged with the crucial obligation of ensuring that the legislative initiatives pursued by our Parliament and legislatures conform to the democratic values expressed in the Canadian Charter of Rights and Freedoms... It is in this latter sense that the current *Morgentaler* appeal differs from the one we heard a decade ago.

While I differ with the Chief Justice in the disposition of this appeal, I would accept his words, referred to above, which describe the role of the Court, but I would suggest that in "ensuring that the legislative initiatives pursued by our Parliament and legislatures conform to the democratic values expressed in the Canadian Charter of Rights and Freedoms" the courts must confine themselves to such democratic values as are clearly found and expressed in the Charter and refrain from imposing or creating other values not so based.

It follows, then, in my view, that the task of the Court in this case is not to solve nor seek to solve what might be called the abortion issue, but simply to measure the content of s. 251 against the Charter. While this may appear to be self-evident, the distinction is of vital importance. If a particular interpretation enjoys no support, express or reasonably implied, from the Charter, then the Court is without power to clothe such an interpretation with constitutional status. It is not for the Court to substitute its own views on the merits of a given question for those of Parliament. The Court must consider not what is, in its view, the best solution to the problem posed; its role is confined to deciding whether the solution enacted by Parliament offends the Charter. If it does, the provision must be struck down or declared inoperative, and Parliament may then enact such different provisions as it may decide. I adopt the words of Holmes J., which were referred to in *Ferguson v. Skrupka*, 372 U.S. 726 (1963), at pp. 729-30:

> There was a time when the Due Process Clause was used by this Court to strike down laws which were thought unreasonable, that is, unwise or incompatible with some particular economic or social philosophy. In this manner the Due Process Clause was used, for example, to nullify laws prescribing maximum hours for work in bakeries, *Lochner v. New York*, 198 U.S. 45 (1905), outlawing "yellow dog" contracts, *Coppage v. Kansas*, 236 U.S. 1 (1915), setting minimum wages for women, *Adkins v. Children's Hospital*, 261 U.S. 525 (1923), and fixing the weight of loaves of bread, *Jay Burns Baking Co. v. Bryan*, 264 U.S. 504 (1924). This intrusion by the judiciary into the realm of legislative value judgments was strongly objected to at the time, particularly by Mr. Justice Holmes and Mr. Justice Brandeis. Dissenting from the Court's invalidating a state statute which regulated the resale price of theatre and other tickets, Mr. Justice Holmes said:
>
> > I think the proper course is to recognize that a state legislature can do whatever it sees fit to do unless it is restrained by some express prohibition in the Constitution of the United States or of the State, and that Courts should be careful not extend such prohibitions beyond their obvious meaning by reading into them conceptions of public policy that the particular Court may happen to entertain.
>
> And in an earlier case he had emphasized that, "The criterion of constitutionality is not whether we believe the law to be for the public good".
>
> The doctrine that prevailed in *Lochner*, *Coppage*, *Adkins*, *Burns*, and like cases — that due process authorizes courts to hold laws unconstitutional when they believe the legislature has acted unwisely — has long since been discarded. We have returned to the original constitutional proposition that courts do not

substitute their social and economic beliefs for the judgment of legislative bodies, who are elected to pass laws.

Holmes J. wrote in 1927, but his words have retained their force in American jurisprudence: see *City of New Orleans v. Dukes*, 427 U.S. 297 (1976), at p. 304, *Minnesota v. Clover Leaf Creamery Co.*, 449 U.S. 456 (1981), at p. 469, and *Hoffman Estates v. Flipside, Hoffman Estates, Inc.*, 455 U.S. 489 (1982), at pp. 504-05. In my view, although written in the American context, the principle stated is equally applicable in Canada.

It is essential that this principle be maintained in a constitutional democracy. The Court must not resolve an issue such as that of abortion on the basis of how many judges may favour "pro-choice" or "pro-life". To do so would be contrary to sound principle and the rule of law affirmed in the preamble to the Charter which must mean that no discretion, including a judicial discretion, can be unlimited. But there is a problem, for the Court must clothe the general expression of rights and freedoms contained in the Charter with real substance and vitality. How can the courts go about this task without imposing at least some of their views and predilections upon the law? This question has been the subject of much discussion and comment. Many theories have been postulated but few have had direct reference to the problem in the Canadian context. In my view, this Court has offered guidance in this matter. In such cases as *Hunter v. Southam Inc.*, [1984] 2 S.C.R. 145, at pp. 155-56, and *R. v. Big M Drug Mart Ltd.*, [1985] 1 S.C.R. 295, at p. 344, it has enjoined what has been termed a "purposive approach" in applying the Charter and its provisions. I take this to mean that the Courts should interpret the Charter in a manner calculated to give effect to its provisions, not to the idiosyncratic view of the judge who is writing. This approach marks out the limits of appropriate Charter adjudication. It confines the content of Charter guaranteed rights and freedoms to the purposes given expression in the Charter. Consequently, while the courts must continue to give a fair, large and liberal construction to the Charter provisions, this approach prevents the Court from abandoning its traditional adjudicatory function in order to formulate its own conclusions on questions of public policy, a step which this Court has said on numerous occasions it must not take. That Charter interpretation is to be purposive necessarily implies the converse: it is not to be "non-purposive". A court is not entitled to define a right in a manner unrelated to the interest which the right in question was meant to protect. I endeavoured to formulate an approach to the problem in *Reference Re Public Service Employee Relations Act*, [1987] 1 S.C.R. 313, in these words, at p. 394:

> It follows that while a liberal and not overly legalistic approach should be taken to constitutional interpretation, the Charter should not be regarded as an empty vessel to be filled with whatever meaning we might wish from time to time. The interpretation of the Charter, as of all constitutional documents, is constrained by the language, structure and history of the constitutional text, by constitutional tradition, and by the history, traditions, and underlying philosophies of our society.

The approach, as I understand it, does not mean that judges may not make some policy choices when confronted with competing conceptions of the extent of rights or freedoms. Difficult choices must be made and the personal views of judges will unavoidably be engaged from time to time. The decisions made by judges, however, and the interpretations that they advance or accept must be plausibly inferable from something in the Charter. It is not for the courts to manufacture a constitutional right out of whole cloth. I conclude on this question by citing and adopting the following words, although spoken in dissent, from the judgment of Harlan J. in *Reynolds v. Sims*, 377 U.S. 533 (1964), which, in my view, while stemming from the American experience, are equally applicable in a consideration of the Canadian position. Harlan J. commented, at pp. 624-25, on the:

> . . . current mistaken view of the Constitution and the constitutional function of this Court. This view, in a nutshell, is that every major social ill in this country can find its cure in some constitutional "principle," and that this Court should "take the lead" in promoting reform when other branches of government fail to act. The Constitution is not a panacea for every blot upon the public welfare, nor should this Court, ordained as a judicial body, be thought of as a general haven for reform movements. The Constitution is an instrument of government, fundamental to which is the premise that in a diffusion of governmental authority lies the greatest promise that this Nation will realize liberty for all its citizens. This Court, limited in function in accordance with that premise, does not serve its high purpose when it exceeds its authority, even to satisfy justified impatience with the slow workings of the political process. For when, in the name of constitutional interpretation, the Court *adds* something to the Constitution that was deliberately excluded from it, the Court in reality substitutes its view of what should be so for the amending process.

The Right to Abortion and s. 7 of the Charter

The judgment of my colleague, Wilson J., is based upon the proposition that a pregnant woman has a right, under s. 7 of the Charter, to have an abortion. The same concept underlies the judgment of the Chief Justice. He reached the conclusion that a law which forces a woman to carry a foetus to term, unless certain criteria are met which are unrelated to her own priorities and aspirations, impairs the security of her person. That, in his view, is the effect of s. 251 of the Criminal Code. He has not said in specific terms that the pregnant woman has the right to an abortion, whether therapeutic or otherwise. In my view, however, his whole position depends for its validity upon that proposition and that interference with the right constitutes an infringement of her right to security of the person. It is said that a law which forces a woman to carry a foetus to term unless she meets certain criteria unrelated to her own priorities and aspirations interferes with security of her person. If compelling a woman to complete her pregnancy interferes with security of her person, it can only be because the concept of security of her person includes a right not to be compelled to carry the child to completion of her pregnancy. This, then, is simply to say that she has a right to have an abortion. It follows, then, that if no such right can be shown, it cannot be said that security of her person has been infringed by state action or otherwise.

All laws, it must be noted, have the potential for interference with individual priorities and aspirations. In fact, the very purpose of most legislation is to cause such interference. It is only when such legislation goes beyond interfering with priorities and aspirations, and abridges rights, that courts may intervene. If a law prohibited membership in a lawful association it would be unconstitutional, not because it would interfere with priorities and aspirations, but because of its interference with the guaranteed right of freedom of association under s. 2(d) of the Charter. Compliance with the Income Tax Act has, no doubt, frequently interfered with priorities and aspirations. The taxing provisions are not, however, on that basis unconstitutional, because the ordinary taxpayer enjoys no right to be tax free. Other illustrations may be found. In my view, it is clear that before it could be concluded that any enactment infringed the concept of security of the person, it would have to infringe some underlying right included in or protected by the concept. For the appellants to succeed here, then, they must show more than an interference with priorities and aspirations; they must show the infringement of a right which is included in the concept of security of the person.

The proposition that women enjoy a constitutional right to have an abortion is devoid of support in the language of s. 7 of the Charter or any other section. While some human rights documents, such as the American Convention on Human Rights, 1969 (Article 4(1)), expressly address the question of abortion, the Charter is entirely silent on the point. It may be of some significance that the Charter uses specific language in dealing with other topics, such as voting rights, religion, expression and such controversial matters as mobility rights, language rights and minority rights, but remains silent on the question of abortion which, at the time the Charter was under consideration, was as much a subject of public controversy as it is today. Furthermore, it would appear that the history of the constitutional text of the Charter affords no support for the appellants' proposition. A reference to the Minutes of the Special Joint Committee of Senate and House of Commons on the Constitution of Canada (Proceedings 32nd. Parl. Sess. 1 (1981), vol. 46, p. 43) reveals the following exchange:

> **Mr. Crombie:** . . . And I ask you then finally, what effect will the inclusion of the due process clause have on the question of marriage, procreation, or the parental care of children? . . .
> **Mr. Chrétien:** The point, Mr. Crombie, that it is important to understand the difference is that we pass legislation here on abortion, criminal code, and we pass legislation on capital punishment; Parliament has

the authority to do that, and the court at this moment, because we do not have the due process of law written there, cannot go and see whether we made the right decision or the wrong decision in Parliament.

If you write down the words, "due process of law" here, the advice I am receiving is the court could go behind our decision and say that their decision on abortion was not the right one, their decision on capital punishment was not the right one, and it is a danger, according to legal advice I am receiving, that it will very much limit the scope of the power of legislation by the Parliament and we do not want that; and it is why we do not want the words "due process of law". These are the two main examples that we should keep in mind.

You can keep speculating on all the things that have never been touched, but these are two very sensitive areas that we have to cope with as legislators and my view is that Parliament has decided a certain law on abortion and a certain law on capital punishment, and it should prevail and we do not want the courts to say that the judgment of Parliament was wrong in using the constitution.

This passage, of course, revolves around the second and not the first limb of s. 7, but it offers no support for the suggestion that it was intended to bring the question of abortion into the Charter.

It cannot be said that the history, traditions and underlying philosophies of our society would support the proposition that a right to abortion could be implied in the Charter. The history of the legal approach to this question, reflective of public policy, was conveniently canvassed in the Ontario Court of Appeal in this case in these terms, at pp. 364-66:

History of the law of abortion.

The history of the law of abortion is of some importance. At common law procuring an abortion before quickening was not a criminal offence. Quickening occurred when the pregnant woman could feel the foetus move in her womb. It was a misdemeanour to procure an abortion after quickening: *Blackstone's Commentaries on the Laws of England*, Book 1, pp. 129-30. The law of criminal abortion was first codified in England in Lord Ellenborough's Act, 1803 (U.K.), c. 58. That Act made procuring an abortion of a quick foetus a capital offence and provided lesser penalties for abortion before quickening. After the Offences Against the Person Act, 1861 (U.K.), c. 10, s. 58, no differentiation in penalty was made in England on the basis of the stage of foetal development. The offence was a felony and the maximum penalty life imprisonment. The Infant Life (Preservation) Act, 1929 (U.K.), c. 34 gave greater protection to a viable foetus by creating the offence of child destruction where a child capable of being born alive was caused to die except in good faith to preserve the life of the mother. In *R. v. Bourne*, [1939] 1 K.B. 687, the prohibition against abortion both at common law and by statute was held to be subject to the common law defence based upon the necessity of saving the mother's life.

The earliest statutory prohibition in Canada against attempting to procure an abortion is to be found in "An Act respecting Offences against the Person", 1869 (Can.), c. 20, ss. 59 and 60. The Act was based on Lord Ellenborough's Act and the Offences Against the Person Act, 1861. The provisions relating to abortion were included in the Canadian Criminal Code in 1892 (1892 (Can.), c. 29, ss. 272 to 274), and with slight changes were included in the Codes of 1906 (R.S.C. 1906, c. 146, ss. 303 to 306); 1927 (R.S.C. 1927, c. 36, ss. 303 to 306) and 1954 (1953-54 (Can.), c. 51, ss. 237 and 238).

Section 251(1) made it clear that Parliament regarded procuring an abortion as a very serious crime for which there was a maximum sentence of imprisonment for life.

In 1969, Parliament alleviated the situation by the addition to s. 251 of ss. (4), (5), (6) and (7) as exculpatory provisions by 1968-69, c. 38, s. 18. These subsections provided that it was not a criminal act to procure an abortion where the continuation of the pregnancy would or would be likely to endanger the life or health of a female person. As can be seen, in order to come within the exceptions to s. 251(1) and (2),

> (a) the majority of the members of a therapeutic abortion committee comprising not less than three qualified medical practitioners of an accredited or approved hospital had to certify in writing after reviewing the case at a meeting that in the opinion of the majority the continuation of the pregnancy would or would be likely to endanger the life or health of a female person;
>
> (b) the abortion had to be performed in an accredited or approved hospital by a medical practitioner to whom the certificate was given who was not a member of the committee.

By defining criminal conduct more narrowly, these amendments reflected the contemporary view that abortion is not always socially undesirable behaviour.

As the Court of Appeal said, the amendments to the Criminal Code which imported s. 251 are indicative of a changing view on this question, but it is not possible to erect upon the words of s. 251 a constitutional right to abortion.

The historical review of the legal approach in Canada taken from the judgment of the Court of Appeal serves, as well, to cast light on the underlying philosophies of our society and establishes that there has never been a general right to abortion in Canada. There has always been clear recognition of a public interest in the protection of the unborn and there has been no evidence or indication of any general acceptance of the concept of abortion at will in our society. It is to be observed as well that at the time of adoption of the Charter the sole provision for an abortion in Canadian law was that to be found in s. 251 of the Criminal Code. It follows then, in my view, that the interpretive approach to the Charter, which has been accepted in this Court, affords no support for the entrenchment of a constitutional right of abortion.

As to an asserted right to be free from any state interference with bodily integrity and serious state-imposed psychological stress, I would say that to be accepted, as a constitutional right, it would have to be based on something more than the mere imposition, by the State, of such stress and anxiety. It must, surely, be evident that many forms of government action deemed to be reasonable, and even necessary in our society, will cause stress and anxiety to many, while at the same time being acceptable exercises of government power in pursuit of socially desirable goals. The very facts of life in a modern society would preclude the entrenchment of such a constitutional right. Governmental action for the due governance and administration of society can rarely please everyone. It is hard to imagine a governmental policy or initiative which will not create significant stress or anxiety for some and, frequently, for many members of the community. Government must have the power to expropriate land, to zone land, to regulate its use and the rights and conditions of its occupations. The exercise of these powers is frequently the cause of serious stress and anxiety. In the interests of public health and welfare, governments must have and exercise the power to regulate, control — and even suppress — aspects of the manufacture, sale and distribution of alcohol and drugs and other dangerous substances. Stress and anxiety resulting from the exercise of such powers cannot be a basis for denying them to the authorities. At the present time there is great pressure on governments to restrict — and even forbid — the use of tobacco. Government action in this field will produce much stress and anxiety among smokers and growers of tobacco, but it cannot be said that this will render unconstitutional control and regulatory measures adopted by governments. Other illustrations abound to make the point.

To invade the s. 7 right of security of the person, there would have to be more than state-imposed stress or strain. A breach of the right would have to be based upon an infringement of some interest which would be of such nature and such importance as to warrant constitutional protection. This, it would seem to me, would be limited to cases where the state-action complained of, in addition to imposing stress and strain, also infringed another right, freedom or interest which was deserving of protection under the concept of security of the person. For the reasons outlined above, the right to have an abortion — given the language, structure and history of the Charter and given the history, traditions and underlying philosophies of our society — is not such an interest. Any right to an abortion will remain circumscribed by the terms of s. 251 of the Criminal Code. I refer to the following passage from the judgment of the court below, at p. 378:

> One cannot overlook the fact that the situation respecting a woman's right to control her own person becomes more complex when she becomes pregnant, and that some statutory control may be appropriate. We agree with Parker A.C.J.H.C. in the court below that, bearing in mind the statutory prohibition against abortion in Canada which has existed for over 100 years, it could not be said that there is a right to procure an abortion so deeply rooted in our traditions and way of life as to be fundamental. A woman's only right to an abortion at the time the Charter came into force would accordingly appear to be that given to her by s-s. (4) of s. 251.

I would only add that even if a general right to have an abortion could be found under s. 7 of the Charter, it is by no means clear from the evidence the extent to which such a right could be said to be infringed by the requirements of s. 251 of the Code. In the nature of things that is difficult to determine. The mere fact of pregnancy, let alone an unwanted pregnancy, gives rise to stress. The evidence reveals that much of the anguish associated with abortion is inherent and unavoidable and that there is really no psychologically painless way to cope with an unwanted pregnancy.

It is for these reasons I would conclude, that save for the provisions of the Criminal Code, which permit abortion where the life or health of the woman is at risk, no right of abortion can be found in Canadian law, custom or tradition, and that the Charter, including s. 7, creates no further right. Accordingly, it is my view that s. 251 of the Code does not in its terms violate s. 7 of the Charter. Even accepting the assumption that the concept of security of the person would extend to vitiating a law which would require a woman to carry a child to the completion of her pregnancy at the risk of her life or health, it must be observed that this is not our case. As has been pointed out, s. 251 of the Code already provides for abortions in such circumstances.

Procedural Fairness

I now turn to the appellant's argument regarding the procedural fairness of s. 251 of the Criminal Code. The basis of the argument is that the exemption provisions of subs. (4) are such as to render illusory or practically illusory any defence arising from the subsection for many women who seek abortions. It is pointed out that therapeutic abortions are available only in accredited or approved hospitals, that hospitals so accredited or approved may or may not appoint abortion committees, and that "health" is defined in vague terms which afford no clear guide to its meaning. Statistically, it was said that abortions could be lawfully performed in only twenty per cent of all hospitals in Canada. Because abortions are not generally available to all women who seek them, the argument goes, the defence is illusory, or practically so, and the section therefore fails to comport with the principles of fundamental justice.

Precise evidence on the questions raised is, of course, difficult to obtain and subject to subjective interpretation depending upon the views of those adducing it. Much evidence was led at trial based largely on the Ontario experience. Additional material in the form of articles, reports and studies was adduced, from which the Court was invited to conclude that access to abortion is not evenly provided across the country and that this could be the source of much dissatisfaction. While I recognize that in constitutional cases a greater latitude has been allowed concerning the reception of such material, I would prefer to place principal reliance upon the evidence given under oath in court in my considerations of the factual matters. Evidence was adduced from the chairman of a therapeutic abortion committee at a hospital in Hamilton, where in 1982 1,187 abortions were performed, who testified that of all applications received by his committee in that year less than a dozen were ultimately refused. Refusal in each case was based upon the fact that a majority of the committee was not convinced that "the continuation of the pregnancy would be detrimental to the woman's health". All physicians who performed abortions under the Criminal Code provisions admitted in cross-examination that they had never had an application for a therapeutic abortion on behalf of the patient ultimately refused by an abortion committee. No woman testified that she personally had applied for an abortion anywhere in Canada and had been refused, and no physician testified to his participation in such an application. In 1982, the Province of Ontario had 99 hospitals with abortion committees. In that year in Ontario, hospitals performed 31,379 abortions and 36 of those hospitals performed more than two hundred in one year. There were 17 hospitals with abortion committees in metropolitan Toronto and they performed 16,706 abortions in 1982, nine of them performing more than one thousand abortions each. In 1982 all ten provinces and both territories had at least one hospital with an abortion committee. The evidence was not as clear as to the situation in rural or more remote areas. It would be reasonable to assume that access to abortion would have been more difficult outside of the principal inhabited areas. This situation, however, is common to the delivery of all health care services. Significantly, the testimony and exhibits entered at trial reflect that even in the more permissive abortion regime in the United States there is a similar problem of access. Ten years after the decision in *Roe v. Wade*, 410 U.S. 113 (1973), only slight gains in access had been made in rural areas. It is also worth noting that the evidence adduced at trial, comparing the respective abortion regimes in Canada and the United States, reveals other significant parallels. For example, there is a close parallel in the two countries concerning such matters as the stage in the pregnancy at which abortions are performed and the procedures used to perform abortions at the respective stages. There is also a high degree of similarity in the two countries regarding the percentages and methods of abortion performed in the crucial early second trimester. In both countries, it appears that many of the problems that have arisen in relation to abortion reflect the more general reality that medical services are subject to budgetary, time, space and staff constraints. With abortion, in particular, matters are further complicated by the fact that many physicians regard abortions as unethical and refuse to perform them. In all, the extent to which the statutory procedure contributes to the problems connected with procuring an abortion is anything but clear. Accordingly, even if one accepts that it would be contrary to the principles of fundamental justice for Parliament to make available a defence which, by reason of its terms, is illusory or practically so, it cannot, in my view, be said that s. 251 of the Code has had that effect.

It would seem to me that a defence created by Parliament could only be said to be illusory or practically so when the *defence is not available in the circumstances in which it is held to as being available*. The very nature of the test assumes, of course, that it is for Parliament to define the defence and, in so doing, to designate the terms and conditions upon which it may be available. The Chief Justice has said in his reasons:

> The criminal law is a very special form of governmental regulation, for it seeks to express our society's collective disapprobation of certain acts and omissions. When a defence is provided, especially a specifically-tailored defence to a particular charge, it is because the legislator has determined that the disapprobation of society is not warranted when the conditions of the defence are met.

From this comment, I would suggest it is apparent that the Court's role is not to second-guess Parliament's policy choice as to how broad or how narrow the defence should be. The determination of when "the disapprobation of society is not warranted" is in Parliament's hands. The Court's role when the enactment is attacked on the basis that the defence is illusory is to determine whether the defence is available in the circumstances in which it was intended to apply. Parliament has set out the conditions, in s. 251(4), under which a therapeutic abortion may be obtained, free from criminal sanction. It is patent on the face of the legislation that the defence is circumscribed and narrow. It is clear that this was the Parliamentary intent and it was expressed with precision. I am not able to accept the contention that the defence has been held out to be generally available. It is, on the contrary, carefully tailored and limited to special circumstances. Therapeutic abortions may be performed only in certain hospitals and in accordance with certain specified provisions. It could only be classed as illusory or practically so if it could be found that it does not provide lawful access to abortions in circumstances described in the section. No such finding should be made upon the material before this Court. The evidence will not support the proposition that significant numbers of those who meet the conditions imposed in s. 251 of the Criminal Code are denied abortions.

It is evident that what the appellants advocate is not therapeutic abortion referred to in s. 251 of the Code. Their clinic was called into being because of the perceived inadequacies of s. 251. They propose and seek to justify "abortion on demand". The defence in s. 251(4) was not intended to meet the views of the appellants and provide a defence at large which would effectively repeal the operative subsections of s. 251. Some feel strongly that s. 251 is not adequate in today's society. Be that as it may, it does not follow that the defence provisions of s. 251(4) are illusory. They represent the legislative choice on this question and, as noted, it has not been shown that therapeutic abortions have not been available in cases contemplated by the provision.

It was further argued that the defence in s. 251(4) is procedurally unfair in that it fails to provide an adequate standard of "health" to guide the abortion committees which are charged with the responsibility for approving or disapproving applications for abortions. It is argued that the meaning of the word "health" in s. 251(4) is so vague as to render the subsection unconstitutional. This argument was, in my view, dealt with fully and effectively in the Court of Appeal. I accept and adopt the following passage from the judgment of that court, at pp. 387-88:

Counsel for the respondent in his attack on s. 251

also argued that the section was void for "vagueness". The argument under this head was that the concepts of "health" and "miscarriage" in s. 251(4) yield an arbitrary application being so vague and uncertain that it is difficult to understand what conduct is proscribed. It is fundamental justice that a person charged with an offence should know with sufficient particularity the nature of the offence alleged.

There was a far-ranging discussion by the respondents' counsel on the concepts of "health" and the meaning of the term "miscarriage"; the way in which courts deal with the "vagueness" in the interpretation of municipal by-laws, and an extensive examination of American authorities.

In this case, however, from a reading of s. 251 with its exception, there is no difficulty in determining what is proscribed and what is permitted. It cannot be said that no sensible meaning can be given to the words of the section. Thus, it is for the courts to say what meaning the statute will bear. Counsel was unable to give the Court any authority for holding a statute void for uncertainty. In any event, there is no doubt the respondents knew that the acts they proposed and carried out were in breach of the section. The fact that they did not approve of the law in this regard does not make it "uncertain". They could have no doubt but that the procuring of a miscarriage which they proposed (and we agree with the trial judge that the phrase "procuring a miscarriage" is synonymous with "performing an abortion"), could only be carried out in an accredited or approved hospital after the securing of the required certificate in writing from the therapeutic abortion committee of that hospital.

Finally, this Court has dealt with the matter. Dickson J. (as he then was), speaking for the majority in *Morgentaler (1975), supra*, in concluding a discussion of s. 251(4) of the Criminal Code, said, at p. 675:

Whether one agrees with the Canadian legislation or not is quite beside the point. Parliament has spoken unmistakably in clear and unambiguous language.

In the same case, Laskin C.J., while dissenting on other grounds, said at p. 634:

> The contention under point 2 is equally untenable as an attempt to limit the substance of legislation in a situation which does not admit of it. In submitting that the standard upon which therapeutic abortion committees must act is uncertain and subjective, counsel who make the submission cannot find nourishment for it even in *Doe v. Bolton*. There it was held that the prohibition of abortion by a physician except when "based upon his best clinical judgment that an abortion is necessary" did not prescribe a standard so vague as to be constitutionally vulnerable. *A fortiori*, under the approach taken here to substantive due process, the argument of uncertainty and subjectivity fails. It is enough to say that Parliament has fixed a manageable standard because it is addressed to a professional panel, the members of which would be expected to bring a practised judgment to the question whether "continuation of the pregnancy... would or would be likely to endanger... life or health."

In my opinion, then, the contention that the defence provided in s. 251(4) of the Criminal Code is illusory cannot be supported. From evidence adduced by the appellants, it may be said that many women seeking abortions have been unable to get them in Canada because s. 251(4) fails to respond to this need. This cannot serve as an argument supporting the claim that subs. (4) is procedurally unfair. Section 251(4) was designed to meet specific circumstances. Its aim is to restrict abortion to cases where the continuation of the pregnancy would, or would likely, be injurious to the life or health of the woman concerned, not to provide unrestricted access to abortion. It was to meet this requirement that Parliament provided for the administrative procedures to invoke the defence in subs. (4). This machinery was considered adequate to deal with the type of abortion Parliament had envisaged. When, however, as the evidence would indicate, many more would seek abortions on a basis far wider than that contemplated by Parliament, any system would come under stress and possibly fail. It is not without significance that many of the appellants' clients did not meet the standard set or did not seek to invoke it and that is why their clinic took them in. What has confronted the scheme has been a flood of demands for abortions, some of which could meet the tests of s. 251(4) and many which could not. In so far as it may be said that the administrative scheme of the Act has operated inefficiently, a proposition which may be highly questionable, it is caused principally by forces external to the statute, the external circumstances being a general demand for abortion irrespective of the provisions of s. 251. It is not open to a court, in my view, to strike down a statutory provision on this basis.

The appellants in this Court raised other arguments, most of which, in my view, may be briefly dealt with.

Section 605 of the Criminal Code

It was contended that s. 605(1)(*a*), giving the Crown a right of appeal against an acquittal in a trial court on any ground involving a question of law alone offended ss. 7, 11(*d*), 11(*f*) and 11(*h*) of the Charter. Reliance was placed primarily on s. 11(*h*). There is a simply answer to this argument. The words of s. 11(*h*), "if finally acquitted" and "if finally found guilty", must be construed to mean *after the appellate procedures have been completed*, otherwise there would be no point or meaning in the word "finally". There is no merit in this ground. I would dispose of this question for the reasons given by the Court of Appeal.

Section 251 of the Criminal Code — violation of s. 15 of the Charter

I find no merit in the argument advanced under this heading to the effect that the equality rights of women are infringed by s. 251 of the Criminal Code and on this issue again I would adopt the reasons of the Ontario Court of Appeal found at 52 O.R. (2d) 392-97.

Section 251 of the Criminal Code and s. 2(a) of the Charter

I am unable to find any abridgement of freedom of conscience and religion in s. 251 of the Criminal Code. I agree with, and on this ground of appeal I would adopt, the reasons for judgment of the Ontario Court of Appeal: (1985), 52 O.R. (2d) 353, at pp. 389-91.

Section 251 of the Criminal Code and s. 12 of the Charter — cruel and unusual punishment

I would reject this argument and again adopt without variation or addition the reasons of the Ontario Court of Appeal: 52 O.R. (2d) 392.

Section 91(27) Constitution Act, 1867 (ultra vires)

It was submitted on this issue that s. 251 was *ultra vires* of Parliament and could no longer be supported under the criminal power because it was colourable legislation in pith and substance, legislation for the protection of health and, therefore, within provincial competence. There is, in my view, no merit in this argument and I again adopt the reasons of the Ontario Court of Appeal: (1985) 52 O.R. (2d) 353, at pp. 397-99.

Section 96 Constitution Act, 1867

The essence of this argument was that s. 251 of the Criminal Code purported to give powers to therapeutic abortion committees exercised by county, district and superior courts at the time of Confederation. There is no merit in this argument. I adopt the reasons of the Ontario Court of Appeal (1985), 52 O.R. (2d) 353, at p. 400.

Wrongful interdelegation of powers

I would dispose of this argument which was to the

effect that s. 251 delegated powers relating to criminal law to the Provinces generally, as did the Court of Appeal in their reasons: (1985) 52 O.R. (2d) 353, at p. 399. I do not wish, however, to say anything about *Re Peralta et al. and The Queen in Right of Ontario* (1985), 49 O.R. (2d), 705, which is relied upon by that court and is currently on appeal to this Court.

Defence of Necessity

This ground of appeal must also fail. There is no evidence whatever in the record that could support the defence.

Counsel's Address

In his reasons for judgment, the Chief Justice referred to defence counsel's address to the jury at trial, in which he had told the jury that they need not apply s. 251 of the Criminal Code if they thought it was bad law. I would associate myself with what the Chief Justice has said on this question. I am in full agreement with him that counsel was wrong in addressing the jury as he did and I would add that such practice, if commonly adopted, would undermine and place at risk the whole jury system.

Conclusion

Before leaving this case, I wish to make it clear that I express no opinion on the question of whether, or upon what conditions, there should be a right for a pregnant woman to have an abortion free of legal sanction. No valid constitutional objection to s. 251 of the Criminal Code has, in my view, been raised and, consequently, if there is to be a change in the law concerning this question it will be for Parliament to make. Questions of public policy touching on this controversial and divisive matter must be resolved by the elected Parliament. It does not fall within the proper jurisdiction of the courts. Parliamentary action on this matter is subject to judicial review but, in my view, nothing in the Canadian Charter of Rights and Freedoms gives the Court the power or duty to displace Parliament in this matter involving, as it does, general matters of public policy.

I would adopt as clearly expressive of the proper approach to be taken by the courts in dealing with Charter issues the words of Taylor J., of the Supreme Court of British Columbia, in the case of *Harrison v. University of British Columbia*, [1986] 6 W.R. 7. The facets of that case concerned the question of mandatory retirement provisions for employees of the University of British Columbia. The question of discrimination under s. 15 was raised. In dealing with the question of the purpose and constitutional effect of the Charter, Taylor J., at p. 11, after noting that the Charter functions assigned to the courts do not "allocate to the courts the responsibility for designing, initiating or directing social or economic policy", continued:

> It is, of course, true that the function of the courts has been extended. In many cases in which the meaning or proper application of the Charter is in doubt the courts must decide whether or not a legislative, administrative or other act complained of requires constitutional sanction, and such decisions may well have social or economic consequences. As has been emphasized by Lamer J. in *Re B.C. Motor Vehicle Act*, [1985] 2 S.C.R. 486 at 496-97, [1986] 1 W.W.R. 481 (sub. nom. *Ref. re* S. 94(2) of Motor Vehicle Act), 69 B.C.L.R. 145, 48 C.R. (3d) 289, 36 M.V.R. 240, 23 C.C.C. (3d) 289, 24 D.L.R. (4th) 536, 18 C.R.R. 30, 63 N.R. 266, this imposes on the courts a new and onerous duty. In carrying out that task, however, the courts can be concerned with social or economic implications only to the extent that they assist in answering the question whether or not the right claimed is one

entitled to constitutional protection. The rights to which the Charter grants protection are those fundamental to the free and democratic society.

This approach is applicable to the abortion question. The solution to this question in this country must be left to Parliament. It is for Parliament to pronounce on and to direct social policy. This is not because Parliament can claim all wisdom and knowledge but simply because Parliament is elected for that purpose in a free democracy and, in addition, has the facilities — the exposure to public opinion and information — as well as the political power to make effect its decisions. I refer with full approval to a further comment by Taylor J., *supra*, at p. 12:

> The present case may serve, perhaps, to emphasize that the courts lack both the exposure to public opinion required in order to discharge the essentially "political" task of weighing social or economic interests and deciding between them, and also the ability to gather the information they would need for that task. When it has run its course the litigation may also have served to demonstrate — if demonstration be needed — that the judicial system of necessity lacks the capacity of parliamentary bodies to act promptly when economic or social considerations indicate that a change in the law is desirable and, of equal importance, to react promptly when results show either that a change made for that purpose has not achieved its objective or that the objective is no longer desirable.

For all of these reasons, I would dismiss the appeal. I would answer the constitutional questions as follows:

1. **Question:**
   Does section 251 of the Criminal Code of Canada infringe or deny the rights and freedoms guaranteed by ss. 2(*a*), 7, 12, 15, 27 and 28 of the Canadian Charter of Rights and Freedoms?

Answer:

No.

2. **Question:**

If section 251 of the Criminal Code of Canada infringes or denies the rights and freedoms guaranteed by ss. 2(*a*), 7, 12, 15, 27 and 28 of the Canadian Charter of Rights and Freedoms, is s. 251 justified by s. 1 of the Canadian Charter of Rights and Freedoms and therefore not inconsistent with the Constitution Act 1982?

Answer:

No answer is required.

3. **Question:**

Is section 251 of the Criminal Code of Canada *ultra vires* the Parliament of Canada?

Answer:

No.

4. **Question:**

Does section 251 of the Criminal Code of Canada violate section 96 of the Constitution Act, 1867?

Answer:

No.

5. **Question:**

Does section 251 of the Criminal Code of Canada unlawfully delegate federal criminal power to provincial Ministers of Health or Therapeutic Abortion Committees, and in doing so, has the Federal Government abdicated its authority in this area?

Answer:

No.

6. **Question:**

Do sections 605 and 610(3) of the Criminal Code of Canada infringe or deny the rights and freedoms guaranteed by ss. 7, 11(*d*), 11(*f*), 11(*h*) and 24(1) of the Canadian Charter of Rights and Freedoms?

Answer:

With respect to s. 605, the answer is No. As to s.

610(3), I adopt the reasons of the Court of Appeal and say that no costs should be awarded.

7. **Question:**

If sections 605 and 610(3) of the Criminal Code of Canada infringe or deny the rights and freedoms guaranteed by ss. 7, 11(*d*), 11(*f*), 11(*h*) and 24(1) of the Canadian Charter of Rights and Freedoms, are ss. 605 and 610(3) justified by s. 1 of the Canadian Charter of Rights and Freedoms and therefore not inconsistent with the Constitution Act, 1982?

Answer:

No answer is required.

Commentary

The Morgentaler Decision:
An Unendorsed Result

Introduction

The result of the four judgments from the Supreme Court of Canada on the constitutionality of section 251 of the Criminal Code is the resounding defeat of an unfair and discriminatory law, and a significant victory for women.

For women, access to abortion is a fundamental issue, and it has been a fundamental issue for many years, not just during this recent period of controversy. It raises, inescapably, the question of whether women are autonomous, independent persons or, as Madame Justice Wilson says, "passive recipients of a decision made by others as to whether [their bodies are to be used to nurture new life]." The pro-choice movement in Canada has been supported by hundreds of thousands of women for whom abortion is not just an important health matter but a basic issue of self-determination. Those who have fought against a criminalized and inaccessible abortion system are women who, whether they will ever have an abortion or not, know that having the right to make choices about reproduction is a fundamental determiner of whether they are free adults in their society.

Canadian women did not live as free and equal adults in our society in the past, and they still do not. Both laws and social traditions have contributed to maintaining the subordination of women. Only a few decades ago married women could not hold property, contract, establish their own residence, hold their own citizenship, or be legal guardians of their own children, and only a few decades ago women could not be doctors, lawyers, or judges, or vote. It is not necessary here to chronicle the continuing inequality women face in professions, employment, family life, and politics. Because of the subject matter of this decision, however, it is important to point out that it is still widely, though often unconsciously, assumed that a woman's sexuality and reproductive capacity is a male possession, not hers independently.

In the *Morgentaler* case, the Supreme Court of Canada was required to address issues fundamental to women's equality and independence. The capacity of Canadian courts to address such issues has been transformed by the addition to our laws of a constitutional protection of rights which never existed before. The Charter of Rights and Freedoms contains new rights and newly framed rights for Canadians. Now the urgent question for women is, Will the courts apply these new constitutional rights so that they will have a real impact on the inequities which women still face?

In order to assist in answering that question, this chapter first examines the analytical steps which all the Supreme Court justices follow in making their decisions in the *Morgentaler* case, and then provides a brief description of each of the four judgments. Next, it analyses the content of the judgments in the light of women's interest in the interpretations of Charter rights, and finally, it considers the future of abortion law and access to abortion in Canada.

Applying the Charter: The Four Judgments

Though the justices differed on many points, there were common steps which they followed in analyzing the constitutionality of section 251 of the Criminal Code, and there was a common body of evidence which all of them considered.

At the risk of some repetition, let us note at the outset that section 251 made it a crime for a woman to have an abortion and for any person to perform an abortion. Anyone who had or performed an abortion was guilty of an offence and was liable to imprisonment.

The defence to the crime of "procuring an abortion", as the law called it, was found in subsection 4 of section 251. It provided that procuring an abortion was not an offence if the abortion was performed by a qualified medical practitioner, in an accredited or approved hospital, after the majority of members of a therapeutic abortion committee had certified that the continuation of the pregnancy would be likely to endanger the life or health of the pregnant woman.

Those were the provisions of the Criminal Code which the Supreme Court measured against the standards of Canada's new Charter of Rights and Freedoms. Although the Court had before them three doctors charged with performing illegal abortions, the focus of their examination was the law's unconstitutional effects on the rights of women. Clearly, this is the issue at the heart of the case; since the doctors' liability is caused by their effort to assist women in this fundamental health matter, the doctors' defence and women's rights to liberty and security of the person are perfectly entangled.

From seven judges, we have four decisions, with the majority of five judges producing three judgments, and the two dissenting judges producing one. All of the judges considered section 7 of the Charter the key one to apply, and each of them followed the same steps in analysing the application of the Charter to section 251 of the Criminal Code. The steps were these:

1. Section 7 rights

Section 7 enunciates rights to life, liberty and security of the person. The first step in the Court's analysis is to determine what the content of these rights is and whether one or more of them is violated by section 251 of the Criminal Code.

2. Principles of fundamental justice

Despite the statement of rights in section 7, the second part of it — "and the right not to be deprived thereof except in accordance with the principles of fundamental justice" — allows those rights to be taken away if it is done in accordance with the principles of fundamental justice. The second step in the Court's analysis therefore is to determine what the principles of fundamental justice are in this case, and whether any deprivation of women's section 7 rights is in accordance with the principles of fundamental justice.

3. Section 1 limitations

Section 1 of the Charter is a general provision which allows that the rights guaranteed in the Charter can be subject to reasonable limits which are demonstrably justified in a free and democratic society. This means that even if a section 7 right is violated, and a woman's deprivation of that right is not in accordance with the principles of fundamental justice, the violation of her right may still be constitutional if it is found to be a reasonable limit under section 1. The third step, then, is to determine whether section 251 of the Criminal Code constitutes a reasonable limit on the rights of women.

In order to find section 251 unconstitutional the Court had to:

1. find that a section 7 right — life, liberty, or security of the person — was violated by section 251, and

2. find that the deprivation of that section 7 right was not in accordance with the principles of fundamental justice, and

3. find that section 251, which causes the violation of section 7, was not a reasonable limit demonstrably justified in a free and democratic society.

And this is what the majority of five judges found.

Though they differed in the emphasis they placed on it, the majority of the judges also agreed on a body of evidence which forms the basis for their judgments. This evidence illuminated the nature of section 251 procedures and their effects on women seeking abortions.

The section 251 procedures required that: 1) a woman apply to a therapeutic abortion committee composed of at least three doctors at an accredited or approved hospital; 2) the committee issue a certificate stating that in the opinion of the majority of its members continuation of the pregnancy would endanger the life or health of the woman; and 3) the certificate be given to a doctor who was not a member of the therapeutic abortion committee who was then authorized to perform the therapeutic abortion.

The majority found that: 1) the effect of these procedures was to restrict the number of hospitals in which abortions can be performed legally; 2) the procedures caused delays in obtaining abortions; 3) the delays were serious and unnecessary; and 4) the delays caused increased risk to women's physical health and increased psychological trauma.

Though the analytical steps required and the basic evidence proven were agreed upon by the majority, their judgments are very different. A brief descriptive look at each one, and at the dissent, provides useful insight into the Court's approach to the abortion issue, and assists in evaluating the impact of the decision.

Dickson and Lamer

Section 7 rights

In the Chief Justice's decision, as in that of Beetz and Estey, security of the person is the key section 7 right examined and applied. Dickson, with Lamer concurring, finds that the right to security of the person is a right to be free from interference by the state with one's body.

Security of the person also protects psychological integrity. In an earlier decision, Lamer found that security of the person encompasses the psychological trauma that is caused by a pending criminal charge. Dickson adopts this reasoning and concludes that "state interference with bodily integrity and serious state-imposed psychological stress, at least in the criminal law context, constitutes a breach of security of the person."

Given this definition of the right, Dickson and Lamer find that section 251 of the Criminal Code amounts to a breach of security of the person for two reasons. The first is, in Dickson's own words: "Forcing a woman, by threat of criminal sanction, to carry a foetus to term unless she meets certain criteria unrelated to her own priorities and aspirations is a profound interference with a woman's body and thus a violation of security of the person." They find, then, that women have the right not to be compelled by the state to carry a foetus to term;

forcing women to do so, with the threat of criminal penalty, is a violation of security of the person. Though Dickson's language casts this finding negatively, McIntyre points out in his dissent that the right not to be compelled by the state to carry a foetus to term is, practically speaking, a right to choose abortion.

The second reason is that the delays caused by the procedures of section 251 themselves endanger women's health and emotional well-being. Having to remit their decision to a therapeutic abortion committee causes substantial delays, and the delays cause increased risk to physical health and increased psychological stress. The delays themselves are therefore a violation of a woman's security of the person.

Principles of fundamental justice

Having found that section 251 violates women's security of the person, both physically and psychologically, Dickson turns his attention to the principles of fundamental justice.

One of the debates about section 7 among legal scholars has been over the depth of review the Court may undertake to determine whether a law or practice complies with the principles of fundamental justice. Is it a review to ascertain whether the content of the law is fundamentally just or a narrower review to determine whether the procedures followed are fundamentally just? Dickson says the principles of fundamental justice have both substantive and procedural content, but that in this case only a review of procedural justice is necessary.

Having examined the procedures of s. 251, Dickson concludes that the combined effect of the requirements is to seriously restrict access to legal abortions. They have the effect of making abortions inaccessible to many Canadian women who are legally entitled to them under subsection 4.

This means that the defence women are offered against a criminal charge for procuring an abortion is unavailable. Dickson says that it is one of the basic principles of a criminal justice system that when Parliament creates a defence, "the defence should not be illusory or so difficult to attain as to be practically illusory." "In the present case," he says, "the structure — the system regulating access to therapeutic abortions — is manifestly unfair. It contains so many potential barriers to its own operation that the defence it creates will in many circumstances be practically unavailable to women who would *prima facie* qualify for the defence..." Dickson concludes that the procedures set out in s. 251 for obtaining a therapeutic abortion do not comply with the principles of fundamental justice.

Section 1 limitations

Section 251, then, is a violation of section 7 as a whole. But is it a reasonable limit on women's section 7 rights within the terms of section 1?

Recently, the Supreme Court of Canada developed a test for assessing when a law constitutes a reasonable limit on rights. This test was first articulated in the case of *Oakes*. The test requires that the objective of the law in question be sufficiently important to justify overriding a constitutionally protected right, and that the means of overriding the right be proportionate to the objective. In determining whether the means are proportionate, the Court considers whether the means 1) are rational, fair and not arbitrary, 2) impair the protected right as little as possible, and 3) have an effect which is proportionate to the objective of the law.

Dickson finds that the objective of section 251 of the Criminal Code is to balance the state's competing interests in protecting the life and health of women and in protecting foetal life, and that this is a sufficiently important objective to allow overriding a constitutional right. However, he says, the means chosen are arbitrary and unfair, they impair women's right to security of the person far more than is necessary, and the effects, far from being proportionate to the objective, defeat the object of protecting the life and health of women because the procedures are so difficult that women may not be able to obtain therapeutic abortions "at least without great trauma, expense and inconvenience." For these reasons, Dickson finds that section 251 of the Criminal Code cannot be saved under section 1.

While the offending provisions of section 251 are found in subsection 4, which provides for therapeutic abortions, Dickson concludes that the whole of section 251 must be found unconstitutional. Section 251 sets out a "comprehensive code" on the issue of abortions and since this code offends section 7, the whole section must be struck down.

2. Beetz and Estey

Section 7 rights

We turn next to the decision of Justice Beetz. Beetz, with Estey concurring, begins from the premise that the right to security of the person includes at a minimum the standard of access to abortion permitted by section 251 of the Criminal Code. That standard requires that when a pregnant woman's life or health is endangered, the interest in her life or health takes precedence over the state's interest in prohibiting abortions. A woman's security of the person, therefore, must mean, at the least, that when her life or health is endangered she will have access to medical treatment without fear of criminal sanction.

Beetz and Estey find that it is the delays caused by section 251 procedures which deprive women of their security of the person. Women's efforts to comply with the requirements of section 251 necessarily cause delays and the delays cause additional medical risks. When state intervention has this effect, it amounts to a violation of women's security of the person.

Principles of fundamental justice

Beetz and Estey find that section 251, when considered as a whole, violates the principles of fundamental justice because it includes rules which are unnecessary, cause risk, and are therefore manifestly unfair.

However, they decide that some parts of the procedures of section 251(4) are valid. The establishment of a standard which indicates when abortions are permitted, the requirement for an independent medical opinion to assure that the standard is met, and some delay to obtain this opinion are allowable. Some state control is appropriate to ensure that abortions are only performed when the mother's life or health is endangered, but, they conclude, the requirements of section 251 are excessive.

Section 1 limitations

Beetz and Estey then turn to the final step of analysis, applying the *Oakes* test to determine whether section 251 can stand as a reasonable limit on a woman's right to security of the person.

Unlike Dickson and Lamer who find that the objective of section 251 is to balance the state's interests in the life and health of the mother and in the protection of the foetus, Beetz and Estey find that the primary objective of section 251 is to protect the foetus. This is a concern, which in their view, is sufficiently important to warrant overriding women's right to security of the person.

However, having already found that some of the rules in section 251(4) are unnecessary and that the practical effect of them is to undermine the health of women, Beetz and Estey find that section 251(4) fails to meet the requirements of the first branch of the proportionality test, namely that the means of achieving the objective must not be arbitrary, or unfair. Section 251, therefore, is not a reasonable limit on the security right of women within the meaning of s. 1.

Thus, Beetz and Estey find: 1) that women cannot be completely denied the right to abortion; 2) the government can, however, impose a standard and require an independent medical opinion to verify that the standard is met, but 3) it cannot create an administrative structure of procedures which results in unnecessary delays and endangers women's health and well-being.

3. Wilson

As Wilson's opening words indicate, she considers it essential to ask different and more fundamental questions and to consider the broad substantive content of both the rights in section 7 and the principles of fundamental justice. "At the heart of this appeal," she says, "is the question whether a pregnant woman can, as a constitutional matter, be compelled by law to carry the foetus to term. . . A consideration as to whether or not the procedural requirements for obtaining or performing an abortion comport with fundamental justice is purely academic if such requirements cannot as a constitutional matter be imposed at all."

Wilson agrees with Dickson, Lamer, Beetz and Estey that section 251 threatens women's physical and psychological security and that this is a violation of section 7. But, she points out, section 7 includes the right to liberty as well as the right to security of the person, and security of the person can mean more than just physical and psychological security. These liberty and security protections, she finds, give a woman the right to choose for herself whether to procure an abortion. Because section 251 violates significant substantive rights in her view, it must be reviewed to determine whether its content is in accordance with the principles of fundamental justice, not just its procedures.

Section 7 rights

The foundation of her decision is the liberty right enunciated in section 7. She finds that the right to liberty means that there are certain parts of each individual's life in which the state cannot interfere. This right is tied to the concepts of human dignity and of individual conscience which are fundamental to a free and democratic society. Wilson finds that "the basic theory underlying the Charter. . . [is] that the state will respect choices made by individuals and, to the greatest extent possible, avoid subordinating these choices to any one conception of the good life. . . . Liberty in a free and democratic society does not require the state to approve the personal decisions made by its citizens; it does, however, require the state to respect them." The right to liberty, therefore, guarantees every individual "a degree of personal autonomy over important decisions intimately affecting their private lives."

The decision to terminate a pregnancy is one of the decisions which comes within the scope of personal liberty. Wilson's words capture the issue best: "This decision is one that will have profound psychological, economic and social consequences for the pregnant woman. The circumstances giving rise to it can be complex and varied and there may be, and usually are, powerful considerations militating in opposite directions. It is a decision that deeply reflects the way the woman thinks about herself and her relationship to others and to society at large. It is not just a medical decision; it is a profound social and ethical one as well. Her response to it will be the response of the whole person."

Having found that the right to liberty protects a woman's right to choose for herself, Wilson considers whether section 251 violates that right and finds that it does. She says that the effect of section 251 is to remove the decision-making from the woman and give it to a therapeutic abortion committee, which as Dickson and Lamer pointed out, decides on the basis of "criteria unrelated to the pregnant woman's priorities and aspirations."

In addition to finding that women's liberty right is violated by section 251, Wilson also finds that it causes a much more fundamental violation of women's security of the person than just the increased risk to health and psychological well-being. Section 251 makes women's child-bearing capacity subject to the control of the state. This is not only an interference with her liberty right to choose; it is also a direct control over her physical person. If the state through its laws can decide whether she must carry a foetus to term, "(s)he is the passive recipient of a decision made by others as to whether her body is to be used to nurture a new life." This, she says, is a profound violation of her security of the person.

Principles of fundamental justice

Having found that section 251 deprives women of their liberty and security rights, Wilson considers the principles of fundamental justice, and in so doing she reviews the content of the law, not just its procedures.

Wilson finds that depriving women of their section 7 rights has the additional effect of infringing their right to freedom of conscience. Freedom of conscience, she says, like freedom of religion, guarantees the right to have beliefs, and to practice them. A woman's decision to terminate a pregnancy is a moral decision, "a matter of conscience," and falls therefore within the scope of section 2 protections. Wilson concludes: "Accordingly, for the state to take one side on the issue of abortion, as it does in the impugned legislation by making it a criminal offence for the pregnant woman to exercise one of her options, is not only to endorse but also enforce, on pain of a further loss of liberty through actual imprisonment, one conscientiously-held view at the expense of another." A deprivation of a section 7 right, which has the effect of violating another right in the Charter cannot, in Wilson's view, be in accordance with the principles of fundamental justice

Section 1 limitations

Can section 251 be saved under section 1? Wilson agrees with Beetz and Estey that the primary objective of section 251 is the protection of the foetus and she considers this a valid legislative objective. The question is, at what point does protection of the foetus become so pressing a concern as to allow the state to overrride women's section 7 rights? Wilson adopts a developmental approach, finding that the value to be placed on foetal life differs depending on the stage of its development. In the early stages of pregnancy, Wilson concludes that women's right to choose for themselves is absolute; in later stages the state could validly examine the reasons for an abortion because of its compelling interest in the protection of the foetus. The precise point at which the state could validly intervene, Wilson leaves to the legislators.

Wilson finds, however, that section 251 does not reflect a developmental approach, but rather takes away all decision-making about abortion from women. "It is a complete denial of the woman's constitutionally protected right under s. 7, not merely a limitation on it." For this reason, she says, it cannot meet the proportionality test in *Oakes* because the means are not proportionate to the objective and it does not impair the right as little as possible. Therefore section 251 is not a reasonable limit, and must be struck down.

4. McIntyre and La Forest

Justice McIntyre and La Forest dissent, finding that section 251 does not violate any Charter rights. They agree that the introduction of the Charter has brought significant changes to the role of the courts, but they warn that the courts must not usurp the role of legislators by passing judgment on the wisdom of legislation, or by creating rights and freedoms which do not have a firm base in the language of the Charter.

In their view, the Charter does not give women a right to abortion. Their reasoning is as follows. First of all, there is no express right to abortion included in the Charter and the absence of an express right is significant since the Charter is specific about other rights, such as voting rights, minority language rights, and mobility rights. Secondly, at the time the Constitution was developed it was not the intent of the legislators that the Charter be used to address the question of abortion. Thirdly, the history of the law in Canada shows that abortion has been prohibited since 1869, and has been an offence under the Criminal Code since 1891. The addition, they say, of subsection 4 to section 251 in 1969, allowing abortions when a woman's life or health is endangered, indicated a change in society's view on the question of abortion, but the fact that the Criminal Code now allows some abortions to be performed legally does not create a right to abortion: " . . . there has never been a general right to abortion in Canada. There has always been clear recognition of a public interest in the protection of the unborn and there has been no evidence or indication of any general acceptance of the concept of abortion at will in our society." Therefore, they conclude, there is no support for a constitutional right to abortion in the language or history of the Charter nor in Canadian legal and social history.

In addition, McIntyre and La Forest disagree with

Dickson's finding that serious state-imposed psychological stress constitutes a violation of the section 7 right to security of the person. They observe that many laws impose stress and anxiety, and yet are appropriate exercises of government's authority to regulate and control. Even if there were a right to an abortion under section 7 of the Charter, McIntyre says it is not clear that section 251 infringes that right, since "there is really no psychologically painless way to cope with an unwanted pregnancy."

Turning to the examination of arguments regarding the principles of fundamental justice, McIntyre and La Forest disagree with the Chief Justice's finding that the defence offered in subsection 4 is illusory or practically illusory. A defence can only be illusory if it is not available in the circumstances in which the law says it will be available. Section 251(4) provides that access to legal abortions will only be provided in very specific, precisely defined circumstances, and there is no evidence to support a finding that in these specified circumstances, they are not available.

They conclude: "This machinery [section 251(4)] was considered adequate to deal with the type of abortion Parliament had envisaged. When, however, as the evidence would indicate, many more would seek abortions on a basis far wider than that contemplated by Parliament, any system would come under stress and possibly fail... What has confronted the scheme has been a flood of demands for abortions, some of which could meet the tests of s. 251(4) and many which could not. In so far as it may be said that the administrative scheme of the Act has operated inefficiently,... it is caused principally by... a general demand for abortion irrespective of the provisions of s. 251. It is not open to a court, in my view, to strike down a statutory provision on this basis."

An Analysis of the Judgments:
Whose Patriarchal Bias is Showing?

Given the patriarchal bias of our legal tradition, it is clear that if the new Charter guarantees are to be meaningful to women, they will have to be given new substantive content rather than being seen as a simple codification of previous legal history and interpretations. The four judgments of the Court are very different, and exhibit a wide spectrum of views and approaches, ranging from the narrow and negative approach of McIntyre and La Forest's dissent to the broad and positive approach of Wilson's judgment. Now that we have surveyed the judgments briefly, let us look at them more analytically to consider what new life the justices have breathed into Charter rights and what substantive content they find in them.

Fortunately, the approach of McIntyre and La Forest did not prevail. They would have had the Court refuse to deal with the Charter as a new instrument with new or newly framed rights. They reason that if there was no right to an abortion before the Charter, there cannot be one now. They point to the history of Canadian law and social custom regarding abortion, reminding us that abortion has been prohibited for more than a hundred years, and they decide that the Charter does not change this tradition nor should it. This stance ignores the efforts that were made by many Canadians to give fundamental protections for Canadians a new design, which would overcome the weaknesses of the Canadian Bill of Rights and be forward-looking. Interestingly, it is also inconsistent with other decisions of the Supreme Court of Canada, such as *Big M Drug Mart Ltd.* and *Therens*, in which the Court stated very clearly that the Charter's rights cannot be interpreted solely by considering the degree to which those rights were enjoyed prior to the

Charter's proclamation. Most importantly, McIntyre and La Forest's logic is entirely defeating for women. 'If it wasn't there then, it can't be here now' means that no departure from patriarchal values is possible. To look only uncritically into the past for insight into the interpretation of rights means that the law must perpetuate discriminatory traditions and preserve the status quo.

Of the majority judgments handed down, Beetz and Estey's is the most narrowly drawn. Their interpretation of section 7 is rooted in a standard already recognized in law, which they find is now incorporated in the Charter; they do not examine the section 7 rights as new and independent from previous history. They find that the standard contained in section 251(4), that is, that abortions are legal when a pregnant woman's life or health is endangered, must be the threshold meaning of security of the person. But in their analysis, Beetz and Estey never move beyond this Criminal Code standard in interpreting security of the person. They find no need to consider whether liberty and security have a larger content, or whether the Criminal Code abortion standard itself infringes women's liberty or security. The standard is clear, they say, and Parliament is entitled to restrict abortions to those which conform to this standard. What Parliament cannot do is create a structure for ensuring that the standard is met which itself creates unnecessary delays and thereby endangers women's health.

At the end of their decision Beetz and Estey make it clear that Parliament could not, in their view, return to the pre-1969 era and make all abortions illegal, as it is pressed to do by the anti-abortion movement. If the standard that the woman's life or health takes precedence when she is endangered is the minimum content of the right to security of the person, prohibiting all abortions would clearly be a violation. Since this is the most conservative of the majority interpretations, it does mean that at the very least the Charter stands as a bulwark against any regression in the law on abortion.

However, there is little in this judgment to give women a sense of firm philosophical ground beneath their feet. It gives no new substantive content to section 7, and it appears clear that another abortion law including the same standard would survive scrutiny by Beetz and Estey if it caused fewer delays.

Dickson and Lamer tread somewhat more firmly into a consideration of the content of section 7. For them, the essence of the breach of section 7 is: "[f]orcing a woman, by threat of criminal sanction, to carry a foetus to term unless she meets certain criteria unrelated to her own priorities and aspirations. . . ." This is not as broad an interpretation as Wilson's but neither is it the strictly procedural approach of Beetz. While Beetz accepts the state-imposed standard which women must meet, Dickson appears to find the standard itself problematic. In the phrase "unless she meets certain criteria unrelated to her own priorities and aspirations", Dickson shows that the fact that a woman cannot choose according to her own needs, and perhaps on grounds other than danger to her life or health, is one of the key elements in his finding the breach of section 7. Though he does not openly or positively state that women have a right to choose, he edges closer to Wilson's position than any of the other justices do.

Dickson's decision also finds that women can not be compelled by the state to carry a foetus to term by threat of criminal sanction. The compulsion and the interference with a woman's body which that compulsion entails are the central pillars on which his analysis rests. This is very different from McIntyre's finding that there is no violation of section 7 at all and from Beetz's decision that it is simply the procedural delays which cause the breach.

However, despite his more substantive reasoning, Dickson's delineation of the right to security of the person is narrow and his definition of the breach of the right is negatively framed. Dickson clearly takes the position that the Charter contains new content, but his decision in this case is cautious, limited in its language, and far less vigorous in tone than some of his other Charter judgments.

Wilson's decision is the most open, the most exploratory and the sweetest to women's ears. Perhaps not surprisingly, she is the only one of the judges who talks about the issue of abortion as though she fully appreciates what it means to women, understanding that, as she says, "[i]t is not just a medical decision; it is a profound social and ethical one as well. [A woman's] response to it will be the response of the whole person."

Wilson maps out a new territory of rights in which this case must be decided, and she is aware of the need to refuse to be bound by the patriarchal traditions of law if women are to be equals in fact. In what may be the first statement of its kind in Canadian judicial history, she says: ". . . the history of the struggle for human rights from the eighteenth century on has been the history of men struggling to assert their dignity and common humanity against an overbearing state apparatus. The more recent struggle for women's rights has been a struggle to eliminate discrimination, to achieve a place for women in a man's world, to develop a set of legislative reforms in order to place women in the same position as men. It has not been a struggle to define the rights of women in relation to their special place in the societal structure and in relation to the biological distinction between the two sexes. Thus women's needs and aspirations are only now being translated into protected rights. The right to reproduce or not to reproduce which is in issue in this case is one such right and is properly perceived as an integral part of modern woman's struggle to assert her dignity and worth as a human being."

For Wilson there is a much more important question here than whether section 251(4) has procedural faults. That question is, of course, do women have the right to choose to terminate a pregnancy? Wilson's decision is founded in a conception of human dignity and worth which, she believes, is the root concept of the Charter and Canadian society. It is the necessary underpinning of a free and democratic society that individuals are valued, that their ability to make "free and informed" decisions is respected, and that they are not treated as means but as ends in themselves. These concepts, of course, are not new; they are the foundation of Western liberal democratic tradition and law. But Wilson's application of these concepts to the issue of women's reproductive freedom, and her conclusion that women have a liberty right to choose abortion and a security right to control their own bodies, are very new to the Canadian judicial scene.

It is unfortunate that Wilson did not take the one additional step, which was open to all the judges, to find that section 251(4) was a violation of women's right to equality in section 15 of the Charter. While Wilson lays all the necessary groundwork for it in her decision, she does not make a finding that being able to control one's own body and make choices about reproduction are rights protected by the equality guarantee. Instead she is silent on this point. For the challenges regarding lack of access to abortion services which may come in the near future, a right to make a choice about abortion based on the equality guarantee may be more useful than a liberty right to choose. Decisions in the United States have found that while women have a liberty right to choose abortion because it is a private matter, they do not have a right to publicly funded abortion services. However, if women have a right to choose based on equality, that equality, it can be argued, cannot be realized unless women also have access to necessary medical services.

Despite this important gap in the analysis, Wilson's decision is unquestionably the strongest. It is the only one which finds broad substantive rights for women in section 7 and articulates them in positive terms. It is also the only one which takes judicial notice of the patriarchal bias in the development of ideas about rights and consciously strives to overcome it.

The Future of Abortion Law and Access

In the aftermath of the Court's decision it is clear that the abortion fight is far from over and that the *Morgentaler* decision, with its strengths and weaknesses, may be an important factor in the struggles to come. Shortly after the decision was handed down the federal government declared that it considered it necessary to rewrite the abortion law, and, unfortunately, the Court's decision, though it struck down section 251 of the Criminal Code, may encourage the government to do that.

Even Wilson, despite her clear and broad statement of women's right to choose, endorses the view that the state has a legitimate interest in the protection of the foetus. In fact, she openly invites government to regulate abortion in the later stages of pregnancy when, she says, the state's interest in the foetus is compelling. This distinction between the early and late stages of pregnancy is based on the theory that the foetus should be viewed in different terms depending on the stage of development, and that, once the foetus can live outside the mother's body, the state's interest in protecting its life can take precedence over the mother's right to choose to terminate the pregnancy.

Though Dickson and Lamer find that the object of s.

251 is to balance the state's interest in the life and health of the mother and the protection of the foetus, all the other judges find that the object of section 251 is to protect the foetus and that this is a valid government objective. Beetz and Estey make it clear that some regulation of abortion is fine and, taken as a whole, the majority decision, despite finding that section 251 is invalid, seems to open the door to regulating abortion again, most likely in the later stages of pregnancy.

Though this seems to be the advice to government, the philosophical groundwork for it is not well laid. The decisions provide no explanation of the interest in the protection of the foetus which they say the state has. All the judges are careful to point out that they are not deciding the separate question of whether the foetus is a person with independent Charter rights, since that is not necessary to this case. Despite their decision to reserve on that point, probably until a case brought by anti-choice advocate Joseph Borowski is heard, they could have provided some explanation of the content of the state's interest in the protection of the foetus since it is part of their analysis of whether section 251 is a valid constitutional limit on rights.

What is the state's interest in the protection of the foetus? It may be difficult for women to discern legitimate meaning in the concept of a state interest in the protection of the foetus, given the history of male control over reproduction, and our society's current lack of value for children. As indicated earlier, historically men have claimed both a woman's sexuality and her reproductive capacity as personal property, and the state has passed and enforced laws which have supported men's right to this control. Now it is necessary to ask, what is the state's interest in the protection of the foetus that is separate from this traditional interest in reinforcing the dominance of men?

Women have little political power in Canadian society, and this makes it difficult to perceive a practical difference between the interests of men and the interests of the state. Since men still control government and the medical profession, any criminal law on abortion will, in practice, tend to reinforce male dominance.

It may be said that the state has a legitimate interest in protecting potential children and members of society, but this rings hollow when women cannot find adequate day care, single parent women are among the poorest people in Canada, and one in six Canadian children is being raised in poverty.

In addition to the fundamental problem of having the state interfere once more in decisions which should be a woman's alone, the regulating of abortions from the date of "viability", as Wilson seems to suggest, holds significant hazards for women. With the development of medical technology, the date of viability is occurring earlier and earlier in a pregnancy. Tying abortion rights to viability dates may result in women's right to choose being eroded again by medical advances. In addition, if pregnant women lose the right to control their own bodies once the foetus is viable, we will see women forced to have caesarian sections, and detained in order to protect the life and health of the foetus. Though these may sound like extreme and unlikely possibilities, such cases have already occurred in the United States and Canada, and could be encouraged by a law which, implicitly or explicitly, gives the state control once the foetus is viable.

Given women's evident interest in giving birth and raising children, and their demonstrated commitment to it, it is hard to understand why the state is a more legitimate or more reliable arbiter of when any abortions should be performed, including late stage abortions, than women themselves are. The government's felt need to control women's choices about abortion indicates that while women are acceptable care-givers, they are not acceptable decision-makers.

At the present time in Canada, the incidence of late stage abortions is very low. Evidence suggests that late stage abortions occur principally because access to early abortions is problematic and because of health crises. There seems little need to regulate these abortions, and every reason to improve access and trust women's decisions. The National Action Committee on the Status of Women and the National Association of Women and the Law, in the wake of the Supreme Court decision, have indicated that they oppose any recriminalization of abortion and are satisfied with the post-*Morgentaler* state of the law. Given the implications of any new abortion law, even one regulating only late abortions, their position seems to be the right one for women.

One of the seemingly attractive reasons given for recriminalizing abortion is that only this will ensure that there is some consistent standard applied across the country. In the division of powers between the federal and provincial governments, criminal law is a federal power and governance of health care is a provincial one. As we have seen, since the *Morgentaler* decision was handed down, there has been confusion among the provinces about what the standard for legal, paid abortions is. Some say that if abortion was recriminalized at least there would be a national standard of access, which it is impossible to guarantee when the issue is in the hands of ten different provincial governments.

The fatal error in this argument is that access was a basic problem when s. 251 was in effect. Indeed, uneven and inadequate access were important reasons that the Court gave for striking section 251 down; recriminalizing abortion cannot solve the access problem.

There is a national standard now, resulting from the

Morgentaler decision; the standard is that a woman has the right to choose to terminate her pregnancy. It logically follows that if the right to choose is to be meaningful, access to abortion services is required. However, the question still remains: will Canadian women be able to obtain abortions or will their right to choose be restricted, now as before, depending on where they live, whether local hospitals perform abortions, and whether they have the money to travel? Access to abortion services, particularly access to early abortions, has been the problem for Canadian women all along. It is difficult to countenance the federal government introducing a new criminal law on abortion, probably to regulate late abortions which women do not want anyway, rather than using its federal spending power in the health field as a lever to ensure that provinces provide access to early, safe, and dignified abortion services.

Given governments' behaviour since the *Morgentaler* decision, the struggle for access to abortion, far from being over, may simply be in another stage. Women may need to go to court again, this time against provincial governments who fail to provide, and pay for, safe accessible abortion services for women. Cases challenging, for example, the complete lack of abortion services for women in Prince Edward Island and ongoing access problems in British Columbia and other provinces, may be in the courts in the coming months.

Unfortunately, it is not easy to predict what the Supreme Court of Canada's approach will be on the access issue because, as we have seen, with the exception of Wilson's, the decisions do not articulate a clear substantive right to choose, and they confine themselves to dealing with the constitutional violation in the criminal law context. Nor is it easy to predict what the Court's approach will be if abortion is recriminalized and new challenges are required.

It would be a pleasure for women if it were no longer

necessary to speculate on the outcome of future decisions of the Court on the abortion issue, and yet it seems clear that it is far from resolved. Unfortunately, while the immediate practical result of the *Morgentaler* decision is precisely the right one, because it makes all abortions legal and gives women the unfettered right to choose, the Court did not openly endorse this result. The Court backed into this result by finding fault, in various ways, with section 251 of the Criminal Code. It did not, except in Wilson's judgment, endorse a clear constitutional right for women to choose. With this unendorsed result, the Court has not given governments a clear instruction to allow women to choose and to make abortion services available. Consequently, we are likely to see new efforts to restrict women's right to choose and insufficient efforts to improve access.

In conclusion, women should feel both elation and concern. This decision is a significant victory because it strikes down a bad law with a solid majority. But it is only a partial victory, because the Court has not clearly endorsed the result, and seems to invite further legislation restricting women's right to choose. In practical terms what is most important is that it does not resolve the access issue, and this means that women will have to continue to struggle.

Shelagh Day
Vancouver, B.C.
May, 1988

APPENDIX: Case Headnotes

(Citation, Summary of Decision, Cases Cited, Statutes and Regulations Cited, Authors Cited)

Supreme Court of Canada

DR. HENRY MORGENTALER
DR. LESLIE FRANK SMOLING
DR. ROBERT SCOTT

v.

HER MAJESTY THE QUEEN
and
THE ATTORNEY GENERAL OF CANADA

CORAM:
The Rt. Hon. Brian Dickson, P.C.
The Hon. Mr. Justice Beetz
The Hon. Mr. Justice Estey
The Hon. Mr. Justice McIntyre

The Hon. Mr. Justice Lamer
The Hon. Mme Justice Wilson
The Hon. Mr. Justice La Forest

Appeal Heard: October 7, 8, 9, 10, 1986
Judgment Rendered: January 28, 1988
Reasons for Judgment by: The Rt. Hon. Brian Dickson, P.C.
Concurred in by: The Hon. Mr. Justice Lamer
Reasons for Judgment by: The Hon. Mr. Justice Beetz
Concurred in by: The Hon. Mr. Justice Estey
Reasons for Judgment by: The Hon. Mme Justice Wilson
Dissenting Reasons by: The Hon. Mr. Justice McIntyre
Concurred in by: The Hon. Mr. Justice La Forest
Counsel at Hearing:
  For the appellants: Mr. Morris Manning, Q.C.
                        Mr. Paul B. Schabas
  For the respondent: Ms. Bonnie J. Wien
                        Mr. W. James Blacklock
  For the intervener: Mr. Edward Sojonky, Q.C.
                        Mrs. Marilyn Doering Steffen

Citation

Trial: (1984), 47 O.R. (2d) 353, 12 D.L.R. (4th) 502, 14 C.C.C. (3d) 258, 41 C.R. (3d) 193, 11 C.R.R. 116.

Appeal: (1985), 52 O.R. (2d) 353, 22 D.L.R. (4th) 641, 22 C.C.C. (3d) 353, 48 C.R. (3d) 1, 17 C.R.R. 223.

r. v. morgentaler

Dr. Henry Morgentaler
Dr. Leslie Frank Smoling

Dr. Robert Scott, *Appellants*

v.

Her Majesty The Queen, *Respondent*

and

The Attorney General of Canada, *Intervener*

indexed as: *r. v. morgentaler*

File No.: 19556.

1986: October 7, 8, 9, 10; 1988: January 28.

Present: Dickson C.J. and Beetz, Estey, McIntyre, Lamer, Wilson and La Forest JJ.

On appeal from the Court of Appeal for Ontario

   Constitutional law — Charter of Rights — Life, liberty and security of the person — Fundamental justice — Abortion — Criminal Code prohibiting abortion except where life or health of woman endangered — Whether or not abortion provisions infringe right to life, liberty and security of the person — If so, whether or not such infringement in accord with fundamental justice — Whether or not impugned legislation reasonable and demonstrably justified in a free and democratic society — Canadian Charter of Rights and Freedoms, ss. 1, 7 — Criminal Code, R.S.C. 1970, c. C-34, s. 251.

   Constitutional law — Jurisdiction — Superior court powers and inter-delegation — Whether or not therapeutic abortion committees exercising s. 96 court functions — Whether or not abortion provisions improperly delegate criminal law powers — Constitution Act, 1867, ss. 91(27), 96.

   Constitutional law — Charter of Rights — Whether or not Attorney General's right of appeal constitutional — Costs — Whether or not prohibition on costs constitutional — Criminal Code, R.S.C. 1970, c. C-34, ss. 605, s. 610(3).

   Criminal law — Abortion — Criminal Code prohibiting

abortion and procuring of abortion except where life or health of woman endangered — Whether or not abortion provisions ultra vires Parliament — Whether or not abortion provisions infringe right to life, liberty and security of the person — Whether or not any infringement in accord with fundamental justice — Whether or not impugned legislation reasonable and demonstrably justified in a free and democratic society.

Criminal law — Juries — Address to jury advising them to ignore law as stated by judge — Counsel wrong.

Appellants, all duly qualified medical practitioners, set up a clinic to perform abortions upon women who had not obtained a certificate from a therapeutic abortion committee of an accredited or approved hospital as required by s. 251(4) of the Criminal Code. The doctors had made public statements questioning the wisdom of the abortion laws in Canada and asserting that a woman has an unfettered right to choose whether or not an abortion is appropriate in her individual circumstances. Indictments were preferred against the appellants charging that they had conspired with each other with intent to procure abortions contrary to ss. 423(1)(*d*) and 251(1) of the Criminal Code.

Counsel for the appellants moved to quash the indictment or to stay the proceedings before pleas were entered on the grounds that s. 251 of the Criminal Code was *ultra vires* the Parliament of Canada, in that it infringed ss. 2(*a*), 7 and 12 of the Charter, and was inconsistent with s. 1(*b*) of the Canadian Bill of Rights. The trial judge dismissed the motion, and the Ontario Court of Appeal dismissed an appeal from that decision. The trial proceeded before a judge sitting with a jury, and the three accused were acquitted. The Crown appealed the acquittal and the appellants filed a cross-appeal. The Court of Appeal allowed the appeal, set aside the acquittal and ordered a new trial. The Court held that the cross-appeal related to issues already raised in the appeal, and the issues, therefore, were examined as part of the appeal. Leave to appeal was granted by this Court.

The Court stated the following constitutional questions:
1. Does s. 251 of the Criminal Code of Canada infringe or deny the rights and freedoms guaranteed by ss. 2(*a*), 7, 12, 15, 27 and 28 of the Canadian Charter of Rights and Freedoms?

HEADNOTES

2. If s. 251 of the Criminal Code of Canada infringes or denies the rights and freedoms guaranteed by ss. 2(*a*), 7, 12, 15, 27 and 28 of the Canadian Charter of Rights and Freedoms, is s. 251 justified by s. 1 of the Canadian Charter of Rights and Freedoms and therefore not inconsistent with the Constitution Act, 1982?

3. Is s. 251 of the Criminal Code of Canada *ultra vires* the Parliament of Canada?

4. Does s. 251 of the Criminal Code of Canada violate s. 96 of the Constitution Act, 1867?

5. Does s. 251 of the Criminal Code of Canada unlawfully delegate federal criminal power to provincial Ministers of Health or Therapeutic Abortion Committees, and in doing so, has the Federal Government abdicated its authority in this area?

6. Do ss. 605 and 610(3) of the Criminal Code of Canada infringe or deny the rights and freedoms guaranteed by ss. 7, 11(*d*), 11(*f*), 11(*h*) and 24(1) of the Canadian Charter of Rights and Freedoms?

7. If ss. 605 and 610(3) of the Criminal Code of Canada infringe or deny the rights and freedoms guaranteed by ss. 7, 11(*d*), 11(*f*), 11(*h*) and 24(1) of the Canadian Charter of Rights and Freedoms, are ss. 605 and 610(3) justified by s. 1 of the Canadian Charter of Rights and Freedoms and therefore not inconsistent with the Constitution Act, 1982?

Held (McIntyre and La Forest JJ. dissenting): The appeal should be allowed and the acquittals restored. The first constitutional question should be answered in the affirmative as regards s. 7 only and the second in the negative as regards s. 7 only. The third, fourth and fifth constitutional questions should be answered in the negative. The sixth constitutional question should answered in the negative with respect to s. 605 of the Criminal Code and should not be answered as regards s. 610(3). The seventh constitutional question should not be answered.

Per Dickson C.J. and Lamer J.: Section 7 of the Charter requires that the courts review the substance of legislation once the legislation has been determined to infringe an individual's right to "life, liberty and security of the person." Those interests may only be impaired if the principles of fundamental justice are respected. It was sufficient here to investigate whether or not the impugned legislative provisions met the procedural standards of fundamental justice and the Court accordingly did not need to tread the fine line between substantive review and the adjudication of public policy.

State interference with bodily integrity and serious state-imposed psychological stress, at least in the criminal law context, constitutes a breach of security of the person. Section 251 clearly interferes with a woman's physical and bodily integrity. Forcing a woman, by threat of criminal sanction, to carry a foetus to term unless she meets certain criteria unrelated to her own priorities and aspirations, is a profound interference with a woman's body and thus an infringement of security of the person. A second breach of the right to security of the person occurs independently as a result of the delay in obtaining therapeutic abortions caused by the mandatory procedures of s. 251 which results in a higher probability of complications and greater risk. The harm to the psychological integrity of women seeking abortions was also clearly established.

Any infringement of the right to life, liberty and security of the person must comport with the principles of fundamental justice. These principles are to be found in the basic tenets of our legal system. One of the basic tenets of our system of criminal justice is that when Parliament creates a defence to a criminal charge, the defence should not be illusory or so difficult to attain as to be practically illusory.

The procedure and restrictions stipulated in s. 251 for access to therapeutic abortions make the defence illusory resulting in a failure to comply with the principles of fundamental justice. A therapeutic abortion may be approved by a "therapeutic abortion committee" of an "accredited or approved hospital". The requirement of s. 251(4) that at least four physicians be available at that hospital to authorize and to perform an abortion in practice makes abortions unavailable in many hospitals. The restrictions attaching to the term "accredited" automatically disqualifies many Canadian hospitals from undertaking therapeutic abortions. The provincial approval of a hospital for the purpose of performing therapeutic abortions further restricts the number of hospitals offering this procedure. Even if a hospital is eligible to create a therapeutic abortion committee, there is no requirement in s. 251 that the hospital need do so. Provincial regulation as well can heavily restrict or even deny the practical availability of the exculpatory provisions of s. 251(4).

The administrative system established in s. 251(4) fails to provide an adequate standard for therapeutic abortion committees which must determine when a therapeutic abortion should, as a matter of law, be granted. The word "health" is vague and no adequate guidelines have been established for therapeutic abortion committees. It is typically impossible for women to know in advance what standard of health will be applied by any given committee.

The argument that women facing difficulties in obtaining abortions at home can simply travel elsewhere would not be especially troubling if those difficulties were not in large measure created by the procedural requirements of s. 251. The evidence established convincingly that it is the law itself which in many ways *prevents* access to local therapeutic abortion facilities.

Section 251 cannot be saved under s. 1 of the Charter. The objective of s. 251 as a whole, namely to balance the competing interests identified by Parliament, is sufficiently important to pass the first stage of the s. 1 inquiry. The means chosen to advance its legislative objectives, however, are not reasonable or demonstrably justified in a free and democratic society. None of the three elements for assessing the proportionality of means to ends is met. Firstly, the procedures and administrative structures created by s. 251 are often unfair and arbitrary. Moreover, these procedures impair s. 7 rights far more than is necessary because they hold out an illusory defence to many women who would *prima facie* qualify under the exculpatory provisions of s. 251(4). Finally, the effects of the limitation upon the s. 7 rights of many pregnant women are out of proportion to the objective sought to be achieved and may actually defeat the objective of protecting the life and health of women.

Per Beetz and Estey JJ.: Before the advent of the Charter, Parliament recognized, in adopting s. 251(4) of the Criminal Code, that the interest in the life or health of the pregnant woman takes precedence over the interest in prohibiting abortions, including the interest of the state in the protection of the foetus, when "the continuation of the pregnancy of such female person would or would be likely to endanger her life or health". This standard in s. 251(4) became entrenched at least

213

as a minimum when the "right to life, liberty and security of the person" was enshrined in the Canadian Charter of Rights and Freedoms at s. 7.

"Security of the person" within the meaning of s. 7 of the Charter must include a right of access to medical treatment for a condition representing a danger to life or health without fear of criminal sanction. If an act of Parliament forces a pregnant woman whose life or health is in danger to choose between, on the one hand, the commission of a crime to obtain effective and timely medical treatment and, on the other hand, inadequate treatment or no treatment at all, her right to security of the person has been violated.

According to the evidence, the procedural requirements of s. 251 of the Criminal Code significantly delay pregnant women's access to medical treatment resulting in an additional danger to their health, thereby depriving them of their right to security of the person. This deprivation does not accord with the principles of fundamental justice. While Parliament is justified in requiring a reliable, independent and medically sound opinion as to the "life or health" of the pregnant woman in order to protect the state interest in the foetus, and while any such statutory mechanism will inevitably result in some delay, certain of the procedural requirements of s. 251 of the Criminal Code are nevertheless manifestly unfair. These requirements are manifestly unfair in that they are unnecessary in respect of Parliament's objectives in establishing the administrative structure *and* in that they result in additional risks to the health of pregnant women.

The following statutory requirements contribute to the manifest unfairness of the administrative structure imposed by the Criminal Code: (1) the requirement that all therapeutic abortions must take place in an "accredited" or "approved" hospital as defined in s. 251(6); (2) the requirement that the committee come from the accredited or approved hospital in which the abortion is to be performed; (3) the provision that allows hospital boards to increase the number of members of a committee; (4) the requirement that all physicians who practise lawful therapeutic abortions be excluded from the committees.

The primary objective of s. 251 of the Criminal Code is the protection of the foetus. The protection of the life and health of the pregnant woman is an ancillary objective. The primary objective does relate to concerns which are pressing and substantial in a free and democratic society and which, pursuant to s. 1 of the Charter, justify reasonable limits to be put on a woman's right. However, the means chosen in s. 251 are not reasonable and demonstrably justified. The rules unnecessary in respect of the primary and ancillary objective which they are designed to serve, such as the above-mentioned rules contained in s. 251, cannot be said to be rationally connected to these objectives under s. 1 of the Charter. Consequently, s. 251 does not constitute a reasonable limit to the security of the person.

It is not necessary to answer the question concerning the circumstances in which there is a proportionality between the effects of s. 251 which limit the right of pregnant women to security of the person and the objective of the protection of the foetus. In any event, the objective of protecting the foetus would not justify the severity of the breach of pregnant women's right to security of the person which would result if the exculpatory provision of s. 251 was *completely* removed from the Criminal Code. However, it is possible that a future enactment by Parliament that would require a higher degree of danger to health in the latter months of pregnancy, as opposed to the early months, for an abortion to be lawful, could achieve a proportionality which would be acceptable under s. 1 of the Charter.

Given the conclusion that s. 251 contains rules unnecessary to the protection of the foetus, the question as to whether a foetus is included in the word "everyone" in s. 7, so as to have a right to "life, liberty and security of the person" under the Charter, need not be decided.

Section 251 is not colourable provincial legislation in relation to health but rather a proper exercise of Parliament's criminal law power pursuant to s. 91(27) of the Constitution Act, 1867. The section does not offend s. 96 of the Constitution Act, 1867 because the therapeutic abortion committees are not given judicial powers which were exercised by county, district and superior courts at the time of Confederation. These committees exercise a medical judgment on a medical question. Finally, s. 251 does not constitute an unlawful delegation of federal legislative power nor does it represent an abdication of the criminal law power by Parliament.

There is no merit in the argument based on s. 605(1)(*a*) of the Criminal Code. It is unnecessary to decide whether or not s. 610(3) of the Criminal Code violates ss. 7, 11(*d*), 11(*f*), 11(*h*) and 15 of the Charter or whether this Court has the power to award costs on appeals under s. 24(1) of the Charter. Whatever this Court's power to award costs in appeals such as this one, costs should not be awarded in this case.

Per Wilson J.: Section 251 of the Criminal Code, which limits the pregnant woman's access to abortion, violates her right to life, liberty and security of the person within the meaning of s. 7 of the Charter in a way which does not accord with the principles of fundamental justice.

The right to "liberty" contained in s. 7 guarantees to every individual a degree of personal autonomy over important decisions intimately affecting his or her private life. Liberty in a free and democratic society does not require the state to approve such decisions but it does require the state to respect them.

A woman's decision to terminate her pregnancy falls within this class of protected decisions. It is one that will have profound psychological, economic and social consequences for her. It is a decision that deeply reflects the way the woman thinks about herself and her relationship to others and to society at large. It is not just a medical decision; it is a profound social and ethical one as well.

Section 251 of the Criminal Code takes a personal and private decision away from the woman and gives it to a committee which bases its decision on "criteria entirely unrelated to [the pregnant woman's] priorities and aspirations."

Section 251 also deprives a pregnant woman of her right to security of the person under s. 7 of the Charter. This rights protects both the physical and psychological integrity of the individual. Section 251 is more deeply flawed than just subjecting women to considerable emotional stress and unnecessary physical risk. It asserts that the woman's capacity to reproduce is to be subject, not to her own control, but to that of the state. This is a direct interference with the woman's physical "person".

This violation of s. 7 does not accord with either procedural fairness or with the fundamental rights and freedoms laid down elsewhere in the Charter. A deprivation of the s. 7 right which has the effect of infringing a right guaranteed elsewhere in the Charter cannot be in accordance with the principles of fundamental justice.

The deprivation of the s. 7 right in this case offends freedom of conscience guaranteed in s. 2(a) of the Charter. The decision whether or not to terminate a pregnancy is essentially a moral decision and in a free and democratic society the conscience of the individual must be paramount to that of the state. Indeed, s. 2(a) makes it clear that this freedom belongs to each of us individually. "Freedom of conscience and religion" should be broadly construed to extend to conscientiously-held beliefs, whether grounded in religion or in a secular morality and the terms "conscience" and "religion" should not be treated as tautologous if capable of independent, although related, meaning. The state here is endorsing one conscientiously-held view at the expense of another. It is denying freedom of conscience to some, treating them as means to an end, depriving them of their "essential humanity".

The primary objective of the impugned legislation is the protection of the foetus. This is a perfectly valid legislative objective. It has other ancillary objectives, such as the protection of the life and health of the pregnant woman and the maintenance of proper medical standards.

The situation respecting a woman's right to control her own person becomes more complex when she becomes pregnant, and some statutory control may be appropriate. Section 1 of the Charter authorizes reasonable limits to be put upon the woman's right having regard to the fact of the developing foetus within her body.

The value to be placed on the foetus as potential life is directly related to the stage of its development during gestation. The undeveloped foetus starts out as a newly fertilized ovum; the fully developed foetus emerges ultimately as an infant. A developmental progression takes place in between these two extremes and it has a direct bearing on the value of the foetus as potential life. Accordingly, the foetus should be viewed in differential and developmental terms. This view of the foetus supports a permissive approach to abortion in the early stages where the woman's autonomy would be absolute and a restrictive approach in the later stages where the state's interest in protecting the foetus would justify its prescribing conditions. The precise point in the development of the foetus

217

at which the state's interest in its protection becomes "compelling" should be left to the informed judgment of the legislature which is in a position to receive submissions on the subject from all the relevant disciplines.

Section 251 of the Criminal Code cannot be saved under s. 1 of the Charter. It takes the decision away from the woman at *all* stages of her pregnancy and completely denies, as opposed to limits, her right under s. 7. Section 251 cannot meet the proportionality test; it is not sufficiently tailored to the objective; it does not impair the woman's right "as little as possible". Accordingly, even if s. 251 were to be amended to remedy the procedural defects in the legislative scheme, it would still not be constitutionally valid.

The question whether a foetus is covered by the word "everyone" in s. 7 so as to have an independent right to life under that section was not dealt with.

Per McIntyre and La Forest JJ. (dissenting): Save for the provisions of the Criminal Code permitting abortion where the life or health of the woman is at risk, no right of abortion can be found in Canadian law, custom or tradition and the Charter, including s. 7, does not create such a right. Section 251 of the Criminal Code accordingly does not violate s. 7 of the Charter.

The power of judicial review of legislation, although given greater scope under the Charter, is not unlimited. The courts must confine themselves to such democratic values as are clearly expressed in the Charter and refrain from imposing or creating rights with no identifiable base in the Charter. The Court is not entitled to define a right in a manner unrelated to the interest that the right in question was meant to protect.

The infringement of a right such as the right to security of the person will occur only when legislation goes beyond interfering with priorities and aspirations and abridges rights included in or protected by the concept. The proposition that women enjoy a constitutional right to have an abortion is devoid of support in either the language, structure or history of the constitutional text, in constitutional tradition, or in the history, traditions or underlying philosophies of our society.

Historically, there has always been a clear recognition of a public interest in the protection of the unborn and there is no evidence or indication of general acceptance of the concept of abortion at will in our society. The interpretive approach to the Charter adopted by this Court affords no support for the entrenchment of a constitutional right of abortion.

As to the asserted right to be free from state interference with bodily integrity and serious state-imposed psychological stress, an invasion of the s. 7 right of security of the person, there would have to be more than state-imposed stress or strain. A breach of the right would have to be based upon an infringement of some interest which would be of such nature and such importance as to warrant constitutional protection. This would be limited to cases where the state-action complained of, in addition to imposing stress and strain, also infringed another right, freedom or interest which was deserving of protection under the concept of security of the person. Abortion is not such an interest. Even if a general right to have an abortion could be found under s. 7, the extent to which such right could be said to be infringed by the requirements of s. 251 of the Code was not clearly shown.

A defence created by Parliament could only be said to be illusory or practically so when the *defence is not available in the circumstances in which it is held out as being available*. The very nature of the test assumes that Parliament is to define the defence and, in so doing, designate the terms upon which it may be available. The allegation of procedural unfairness is not supported by the claim that many women wanting abortions have been unable to get them in Canada because the failure of s. 251(4) to respond to this need. This machinery was considered adequate to deal with the type of abortion Parliament had envisaged. Any inefficiency in the administrative scheme is caused principally by forces external to the statute — the general demand for abortion irrespective of the provisions of s. 251. A court cannot strike down a statutory provision on this basis.

Section 605(1)(*a*), which gives the Crown a right of appeal against an acquittal in a trial court on any ground involving a question of law alone, does not offend ss. 11(*d*), 11(*f*) and 11(*h*) of the Charter. The words of s. 11(*h*), "if finally acquitted" and "if finally found guilty", must be construed to mean after the appellate procedures have been completed, otherwise there would be no point or meaning in the word "finally".

Section 251 did not infringe the equality rights of women, abridge freedom of religion or inflict cruel or unusual punishment. The section was not in pith and substance legislation for the protection of health and therefore within provincial competence but rather was validly enacted under the federal criminal law power. There was no merit to the arguments that s. 251 purported to give powers to therapeutic abortion committees exercised by county, district, and superior courts at the time of Confederation or that it delegated powers relating to criminal law to the provinces generally. No evidence supported the defence of necessity.

Per Curiam: In a trial before judge and jury, the judge's role is to state the law and the jury's role is to apply the law to the facts of the case. To encourage a jury to ignore a law it does not like could not only lead to gross inequities but could also irresponsibly disturb the balance of the criminal law system. It was quite simply wrong to say to the jury that if they did not like the law they need not enforce it. Such practice, if commonly adopted, would undermine and place at risk the whole jury system.

Cases Cited

By Dickson C.J.

Referred to: *Morgentaler v. The Queen*, [1976] 1 S.C.R. 616; *Roe v. Wade*, 410 U.S. 113 (1973); *Paton v. United Kingdom* (1980), 3 E.H.R.R.; *The Abortion Decision of the Federal Constitutional Court - First Senate - of the Federal Republic of Germany*, February 25, 1975, translated and reprinted in (1976), 9 John Marshall J. Prac. and Proc. 605; *R. v. Big M Drug Mart Ltd.*, [1985] 1 S.C.R. 295; *Hunter v. Southam Inc.*, [1984] 2 S.C.R. 145; *R. v. Therens*, [1985] 1 S.C.R. 613; *Singh v. Minister of Employment and Immigration*, [1985] 1 S.C.R. 177; *Re B.C. Motor Vehicle Act*, [1985] 2 S.C.R. 486; *R. v. Jones*, [1986] 2 S.C.R. 284; *R. v. Caddedu* (1982), 40 O.R. (2d) 128; *R. v. Videoflicks Ltd.*, (1984), 48 O.R. (2d) 395; *Mills v. The Queen*, [1986] 1 S.C.R. 863; *R. v. Oakes*, [1986] 1 S.C.R. 103; *Joshua v. The Queen*, [1955] A.C. 121; *R. v. Shipley*, (1784), 4 Dougl. 74, 99 E.R. 774; *United States v. Dougherty*, 473 F.2d 1113 (1972).

By Beetz J.

Considered: *Morgentaler v. The Queen*, [1976] 1 S.C.R. 616; *United States v. Vuitch*, 402 U.S. 62 (1971); referred to:

Singh v. Minister of Employment and Immigration, [1985] 1 S.C.R. 177; *Re B.C. Motor Vehicle Act*, [1985] 2 S.C.R. 486; *Law Society of Upper Canada v. Skapinker*, [1984] 1 S.C.R. 357; *Collin v. Lussier*, [1983] 1 F.C. 213, rev'd [1985] 1 F.C. 124; *R. v. Jones*, [1986] 2 S.C.R. 284; *City of Akron v. Akron Center for Reproductive Health, Inc.*, 462 U.S. 416 (1983); *R. v. Oakes*, [1986] 1 S.C.R. 103; *R. v. Edwards Books and Art Ltd.*, [1986] 2 S.C.R. 713; *Schneider v. The Queen*, [1982] 2 S.C.R. 112; *Mezzo v. The Queen*, [1986] 1 S.C.R. 802.

By Wilson J.

Referred to: *Singh v. Minister of Employment and Immigration*, [1985] 1 S.C.R. 177; *R. v. Big M Drug Mart Ltd.*, [1985] 1 S.C.R. 295; *R. v. Oakes*, [1986] 1 S.C.R. 103; *R. v. Jones*, [1986] 2 S.C.R. 284; *Law Society of Upper Canada v. Skapinker*, [1984] 1 S.C.R. 357; *Meyer v. Nebraska*, 262 U.S. 390 (1923); *Pierce v. Society of Sisters*, 268 U.S. 510 (1925); *Skinnner v. Oklahoma*, 316 U.S. 535 (1942); *Griswold v. Connecticut*, 381 U.S. 479 (1965); *Eisenstadt v. Baird*, 405 U.S. 438 (1972); *Loving v. Virginia*, 388 U.S. 1 (1967); *Roe v. Wade*, 410 U.S. 113 (1973); *Doe v. Bolton*, 410 U.S. 179 (1973); *City of Akron v. Akron Centre for Reproductive Health, Inc.*, 462 U.S. 416 (1976); *Thornburgh v. American College of Obstetricians and Gynecologists*, 106 S. Ct. 2169 (1986); *Mills v. The Queen*, [1986] 1 S.C.R. 863; *Re B.C. Motor Vehicle Act*, [1985] 2 S.C.R. 486; *R. v. Lyons*, [1987] 2 S.C.R. 309.

By McIntyre J. (dissenting)

Morgentaler v. The Queen, [1976] 1 S.C.R. 616; *Ferguson v. Skrupka*, 372 U.S. 726 (1963); *New Orleans v. Dukes*, 427 U.S. 297 (1976); *Minnesota v. Clover Leaf Creamery Co.*, 449 U.S. 456 (1981); *Hoffman Estates v. The Flipside, Hoffman Estates, Inc.*, 455 U.S. 489 (1982); *Hunter v. Southam Inc.*, [1984] 2 S.C.R. 145; *R. v. Big M Drug Mart Ltd.*, [1985] 1 S.C.R. 295; *Reference Re Public Service Employee Relations Act*, [1987] 1 S.C.R. 313; *Reynolds v. Sims*, 377 U.S. 533 (1964); *Roe v. Wade*, 410 U.S. 113 (1973); *Re Peralta and The Queen in Right of Ontario* (1985), 49 O.R. (2d) 705; *Harrison v. University of British Columbia*, [1986] 6 W.W.R. 7.

Statutes and Regulations Cited

Abortion Act, 1967, C. 87, s. 1(1)(a) (U.K.)

Canadian Bill of Rights, R.S.C. 1970, App. III, s. 1(*b*).

Canadian Charter of Rights and Freedoms, ss. 1, 2 (*a*), (*d*), 7, 8-14, 11(*b*), (*d*), (*f*), (*h*), 12, 15, 24(1), 27, 28.

Civil Code of Lower Canada, art. 19

Code de la santé publique, ss. 162-1. 162-12 (France).

Code pénal, s. 317 (France).

Code pénal suisse, art. 120(1).

Constitution Act, 1867, s. 91(27), 96.

Constitution Act, Preamble, 1982, s. 52(1).

Crimes Act 1961, as amended by the Crimes Amendment Act 1977 and the Crimes Amendment Act 1978, s. 187A(1)(*a*), (4) (New Zealand).

Criminal Code, as amended by the Fifteenth Criminal Law Amendment Act (1976), ss. 218a(1), 219 (West Germany).

Criminal Code, s. 251(1), (2), (3)(*a*), (*b*), (*c*), (4)(*a*), (*b*), (*c*), (*d*), (5)(*a*), (*b*), (6), (7), 423(1)(*d*), 605(1)(*a*), 610(3).

Criminal Law Amendment Act, 1968-69, S.C. 1968-69, c. 37

Criminal Law Consolidation Act, 1935-1975, s. 82a(1)(*a*)(i) (South Australia).

Criminal Law Consolidation Act and Ordinance, s. 79 A(3)(a) (Australian Northern Territory).

Penal Law, 5737-1977 (as amended), ss. 315, 316(*a*)(4) (Israel).

O. Reg. 248/70, now R.R.O. 1980, Reg. 865, under The Public Hospitals Act, R.S.O. 1960, c. 322.

United States Constitution, 14th and 15th Amendments.

Authors Cited

Burrows, Noreen. "Internation Law and Human Rights: The Case of Women's Rights". In Tom Campbell, *et al.*, eds., *Human Rights: From Rhetoric to Reality*. Oxford: Basil Blackwell, 1986.

Canada. Department of Justice. *Report of the Committee*

*on the Operation of the Abortion Law (Badgley
Report)*. Ottawa: Minister of Supply and Services,
1977.

Canada. Law Reform Commission. Fetal Status Working
Group Protection of Life Project. *Options for Abortion
Policy Reform: A Consultation Document*. Ottawa
(unpublished), 1986.

Canada. Law Reform Commission. Working Paper 27.
The Jury in Criminal Trials. Ottawa: Law Reform
Commission, 1980.

Canada. Statistics Canada. *Basic Facts on Therapeutic
Abortions, Canada: 1982*. Ottawa: Minister of Supply
and Services, 1983.

Canada. Statistics Canada. *Therapeutic abortions, 1982*.
Ottawa: Minister of Supply and Services, 1984.

Canada. Statistics Canada. *Therapeutic abortions 1985*.
Ottawa: Minister of Supply and Services, 1986.

Cates, Willard, Jr. and David A. Grimes. "Deaths from
Second Trimester Abortion by Dilation and Evacua-
tion: Causes, Prevention, Facilities" (1981), 58
Obstetrics and Gynecology 401.

Cook, Rebecca J. and Bernard M. Dickens. *Abortion
Laws in Commonwealth Countries*. Granchamp,
France: World Health Organization, 1979.

Cook, Rebecca J. and Bernard M. Dickens. *Emerging
Issues in Commonwealth Abortion Laws, 1982*.
London: Commonwealth Secretariat, 1983.

Garrant, Patrice. "Fundamental Freedoms and Natural
Justice." In *The Canadian Charter of Rights and
Freedoms: Commentary*. Edited by Walter S.
Tarnopolsky and Gerald-A. Beaudoin. Toronto:
Carswells, 1982.

Isaacs, Natalie Fochs. "Abortion and the Just Society"
(1970), 5 *R.J.T.* 27.

Isaacs, Stephen L. "Reproductive Rights 1983: An International Survey" (1982-83), 14 *Columbia Human
Rights Law Rev.* 311.

Joad, C.E.M. *Guide to the Philosophy of Morals and
Politics*. London: Victor Gollancz Ltd., 1938.

MacCormick, Neil. *Legal Right and Social Democracy:
Essays in Legal and Political Philosophy*. Oxford:
Clarendon Press, 1982.

Macdonald. "Procedural Due Process in Canadian Constitutional Law," 39 *U. Fla. L. Rev.* 217 (1987).

Ontario. Ministry of Health. *Report on Therapeutic Abortion Services in Ontario (Powell Report).* Toronto: (unpublished). 1987.

Organization of American States. Inter-American Specialized Conference on Human Rights. "American Convention on Human Rights," Doc. 65 (English) Rev. 1 Corr. 2, January 7, 1970. Original: Spanish. OAS Official Records, OEA/Ser.K/xvl/1.1 (English).

Sumner, L. W. *Abortion and Moral Theory.* Princeton: Princeton University Press, 1981.

Tribe, Lawrence H. *American Constitutional Law.* Mineola, N.Y.: Foundation Press, 1978.

Tyler, Carl W., Jr. *et al.* "Second Semester Induced Abortion in the United States", Cases on Appeal, vol. xxii, p. 4601.

Whyte, John D. "Fundamental Justice: The Scope and Application of Section 7 of the Charter." In Canadian Institute for the Administration of Justice, *The Canadian Charter of Rights and Freedoms* (n.d.)

APPEAL from a judgment of the Ontario Court of Appeal (1985), 52 O.R. (2d) 353, 22 D.L.R. (4th) 641, 22 C.C.C. (3d) 353, 48 C.R. (3d) 1, 17 C.R.R. 223, setting aside from an acquittal found by Parker A.C.J.H.C. sitting with jury (1984), 47 O.R. (2d) 353, 12 D.L.R. (4th) 502, 14 C.C.C. (3d) 258, 41 C.R. (3d) 193, 11 C.R.R. 116. Appeal allowed, McIntyre and La Forest JJ. dissenting. The appeal should be allowed and the acquittals restored. The first constitutional question should be answered in the affirmative as regards s. 7 only and the second in the negative as regards s. 7 only. The third, fourth and fifth constitutional questions should be answered in the negative. The sixth constitutional question should be answered in the negative with respect to s. 605 of the Criminal Code and should not be answered as regards s. 610(3). The seventh constitutional question should not be answered.

Morris Manning, Q.C., and *Paul B. Schabas,* for the appellants.

Bonnie J. Wien and *W. James Blacklock,* for the respondent.

Edward R. Sojonky, Q.C., and *Marilyn Doering Steffen*, for the intervener.

Solicitor for the appellants: *Morris Manning*, Toronto.

Solicitor for the respondent: Attorney General for Ontario, Toronto.

Solicitor for the intervener: *Frank Iacobucci*, Ottawa.

Shelagh Day was the Director of the Saskatchewan Human Rights Commission and the first president of the Women's Legal Education and Action Fund. She currently works with the Canadian Disability Rights Council.

Stan Persky teaches in the philosophy and political studies departments at Capilano College in North Vancouver, B.C., and is a member of the board of directors of the British Columbia Civil Liberties Association.

Other recent New Star titles

SHRINK RESISTANT The Struggle Against Psychiatry in Canada *Edited by Bonnie Burstow and Don Weitz.* Through interviews, journal entries, poetry, graphics, and personal narratives, 40 current and former psychiatric inmates relate their experiences inside the walls of mental hospitals and at the hands of psychiatrists. 260 pages. **$11.95**

FREE TRADE AND THE NEW RIGHT AGENDA *by John W. Warnock.* The Free Trade Agreement and how it fits into business's response to the crisis in the world's capitalist economies since the 1970's. 324 pages. **$11.95**

NO WAY TO LIVE Poor Women Speak Out *by Sheila Baxter.* Fifty women talk about their poverty. Includes statistical information on poverty and women, as well as a directory of anti-poverty and women's groups in Canada. 231 pages. **$9.95**

HASTINGS AND MAIN Stories from an Inner City Neighbourhood *Interviews by Laurel Kimbley; Edited by Jo-Ann Canning-Dew.* Reminiscences of twenty long-time residents of Vancouver's Downtown Eastside upset many of the stereotypes about "skid road". 158 pages. **$9.95**

BEING PREGNANT Conversations with Women *by Daphne Morrison.* Fifteen women speak frankly about their pregnancies. "Incredibly moving." — Sheila Kitzinger. 201 pages. **$9.95**

To order, send cheque or money order to New Star Books Ltd. Price shown includes shipping & handling.

For a free catalogue containing a complete list of New Star titles, write to the address below:

New Star Books Ltd.
2504 York Avenue
Vancouver, B.C.
CANADA V6K 1E3